pacific
flavours

SECOND EDITION

Formac Publishing Company Limited acknowledges the support of the Cultural Affairs Section, Nova Scotia Department of Tourism and Culture. We acknowledge the financial support of the Government of Canada through the Book Publishing Industry Development Program (BPIDP) for our publishing activities.

This book is dedicated to my loving and supportive family: Mel, Kate, David and Elizabeth Lee.

National Library of Canada Cataloguing in Publication

Lee, Virginia, 1947-
    Pacific flavours : guidebook & cookbook / Virginia Lee ; photography by Hamid Attie. — 2nd ed.

Includes index.
ISBN 0-88780-596-5

    1. Cookery—British Columbia. 2. Restaurants—British Columbia—Guidebooks. I. Title.

TX715.6.L43 2004   641.59711   C2003-902284-6

All photos by Hamid Attie with the following exceptions:
Pages 54, 94 (Butchart Gardens; Bonnie Burton); 85 (Whistler Resort; Paul Morrison); 85 Whistler Resort; 103 (Whistler Resort, Greg Griffith); 125 (Fairmont Hot Springs Resort; 134, top and middle (Al Harvey); 134 bottom left (Sumac Ridge Estate Winery); 134 right (Cedar Creedk Estate Winery); 135 (Naramata Heritage Inn); 136 (Quail's Gate Estate Winery); 140 right (Le Crocodile); 141 (L'Emotion Restaurant; 142 left (Raincity Grill; 144 (Circolo); 146 (Café Brio); 147 (J.K. Lawrence); 154 Bearfoot Bistro.
Also pages 29, 30, 31, 35, 47, 65, 105, 117, 129 (various sources).

Formac Publishing Company Limited
5502 Atlantic Street
Halifax, Nova Scotia
B3H 1G4
www.formac.ca

Printed in the People's Republic of China

pacific
flavours

SECOND EDITION

A Guidebook & Cookbook
VIRGINIA LEE

Formac Publishing Company Limited, Halifax

CONTENTS

INTRODUCTION *6*

MAPS *8*

APPETIZERS *10*

Grilled Fanny Bay Oysters with Smoked Paprika Mayonnaise, *12*   Fresh-Shucked Pacific Oysters with West Coast Splash, *13*   Thai Curry Beef with Ginger Aïoli and Avocado on Hearts of Romaine, *14*   Pan-Seared Camembert with Spicy Cranberry Sauce, *16*   Wild B.C. Sockeye Salmon on Red Shiso and Sesame Pancakes, *18*   Nori-Wrapped Dungeness Crab Cakes with Lemongrass Cream, *20* Rare Ahi Tuna with Asian Papaya Slaw, *22*   Baked Artichokes with Garlic Mayonnaise, *23*   Tojo's Golden Roll, *24*

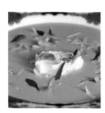

SOUPS *26*

Lobster Bisque, *28*   Leek and Fennel Soup, *29*   Double-Strength Chicken Stock, *30* Sweet Red Pepper Soup, *31*   Sweet Pea Soup with Crème Fraîche and Handpeeled Shrimp, *32*   Noggin's Chowder, *34*   Cayman Island Chowder, *35*   Indonesian Sweet Potato, Coconut and Peanut Soup, *36*   Cream of Chanterelle Soup with Blueberry Crème Fraîche, *37*   Hot-and-Sour Soup, *38*   Vichyssoise with Lobster Medallions, *39*   Smoked Gouda Soup, *40*   Carrot and Sage Velouté, *41*   Pacific Oyster Stew, *42*

SALADS *44*

Edgewater Salad, *46*   Green and Yellow Bean Salad with a Warm Bacon Vinaigrette, *47*   Spinnakers Mixed Greens with Raspberry Vinaigrette, *48*   Spicy Mesclun with Avocado, Mango and Stilton Cheese, *50*   Caprese Salad of Tomatoes and Bocconcini, *51*   Cambozola Caldo Con Crostini, *52*   Sunomono Salad, *54* Cellar Door Caesar, *55*   Spinach Salad with Honey Dressing and Pancetta Feta Tuques, *56*

ENTRÉES *58*

Cinnamon Chili Rub Flank Steak, *60*   Smoked Pork Tenderloin with Oven-Dried Damson Plums, *61*   Chanterelle-Stuffed Venison Medallions with Three-Peppercorn Soy Vinaigrette, *62*   Roasted Garlic Chicken and Grilled Vegetables, *63* Chicken Curry, *64*   Coq Au Vin with Braised Greens, *65*   Herb-Crusted Rack of

Lamb, *66* Smoked Salmon-Stuffed Chicken Breast in Phyllo with Sour Cherry Ginger Glaze, *67* Cranberry-Stuffed Pork Tenderloin in Phyllo, *68* Veal with Lemon Caper Sauce, *69* Edgewater Marinated Venison Medallions, *70* Hay-Roasted Fraser Valley Poussins with Creamy Parmesan Polenta, *71* Braised Rabbit with Wild Mushrooms, Fresh Herbs and Mascarpone Polenta, *72*

SEAFOOD ENTRÉES *74*

Halibut Poêle with Lemon Potatoes and Chive Butter Sauce, *76* 1912 Scallop and Prawn Sauté, *77* Scallops Napoleon, *78* Al Granchio (Black Squid Pasta with Dungeness Crab Sauce), *80* Seared Medallion of Smoked Alaskan Black Cod with Potato Artichoke Hash and Scallion Oil, *81* Grilled Halibut T-Bone with Summer Vegetable Salad and Crème Fraîche Mousse, *82* Coconut Milk and Masala Mussels, *83* Branzio Alla Crosta (Crusted Sea Bass), *84* Almond Ginger-Crusted Chilean Sea Bass with Orange Lime Beurre Blanc, *85* Pan-Charred Rare Tuna with Grotto-Style Sesame Sauce, *86* Sooke Harbour House Steamed Skate Wing with Cranberry Vinegar Sauce, *87* Smoked Black Alaska Cod with Grainy Mustard Dill Beurre Blanc, *88* Cedar-Infused B.C. Salmon with Onion Confit and Hazelnut and Balsamic Vinaigrette, *90* Cin Cin Poached Salmon With Sorrel Sauce, *92* Grilled Fillet of Wild Salmon with Summer Salsa, *94* Stilton-Crusted Salmon Fillet with Warm Caper Relish and Sweet Soy Glaze, *95* Wild Salmon and Sorrel with Fresh Ginger Juice Sauce, *96* Good Night Salmon, *97* Brioche and 7 C's Spice-Crusted Pacific Lingcod, *98*

LUNCH, TEA, BREAKFAST *100*

Orange Cardamom French Toast, *102* Chateau Whistler Granola, *103* Frittata Trattoria, *104* Summerhill Smoked Salmon Eggs Benedict, *105* Spring Mushroom Cannelloni, *106* Sun-Dried Tomato Risotto, *107* Portobello Mushroom Cutlets with Balsamic Sauce and Roasted Baby Vegetables, *108* Chanterelle and Sweet Corn Risotto, *110* Mount Currie Rhubarb and Sweet Ginger Chutney, *111* Empress Scones, *112* Almond Crackers, *113*

DESSERTS *114*

Sunburnt Lemon Pie, *116* Stone Fruit Clafouti with Toasted Hazelnuts, *117* Fresh Berries with Ginger-Scented Mascarpone, Citrus Curd and Pistachio Tuile Towers, *118* Warm Rain Forest Crunch Banana with Hot Chocolate Sauce, *120* Rhubarb Upside-Down Cakes, *121* Stilton Cheesecake with Rhubarb Compote, *122* Chocolate Terrine, *124* Nanaimo Bars, *125* Caramelized Apple and Phyllo Tower with Crème Anglaise and Easy Caramel Sauce, *126* Boca Negra, *128* Frangelico Mousse with Champagne Sabayon, *129* Warm Pecan Pie with Vanilla Bean Ice Cream, *130* Delight of the King, *131*

PROFILES *132*

BC Rockies and Kootenays, *132* Okanagan Valley, *134* Vancouver and Environs, *138* Victoria and the Gulf Islands, *145* Whistler Resort Area, *153*

INDEX *158*

INTRODUCTION

From its southern border shared with the United States to its northern reaches in the subarctic, and from the Rocky Mountains in the east to the vast Pacific Ocean in the west, British Columbia is a magnificent province. Encompassing ninety-five million hectares and with a 7,000-kilometre coastline, it is a land of diverse yet harmonious contrasts.

As I travelled throughout British Columbia by air, road and sea to research and revise this book, the sheer raw beauty of the natural environment constantly struck me. On one flight into Vancouver, the sky below was like a blanket of cotton batting penetrated only by jagged mountain peaks. On another flight, the sparkling Pacific Ocean was dotted with islands as far as the eye could see. I never tired of driving the roads — the Sea to Sky Highway from North Vancouver to Whistler and beyond, the mountain climb through the Coquihalla Pass, the unnamed narrow road perched high above the mighty Fraser River in Cariboo country. And heading out on the ferries that ply the coast gave me a greater appreciation of the sometimes serene, sometimes explosive power of the sea. The views from all these perspectives are simply spectacular: they have to be seen to be believed.

Along the seafood-rich coastal area, warmed by the Japanese current and protected by the mountains, you find the mildest and wettest climate in Canada. In the Fraser River delta, to the south and east of Vancouver, farmers tend animals and plants on a nutrient-rich belt of land. Eastward over the Cascade Mountains is the Okanagan Valley. Its semi-arid climate, with its hot summer weather and long daylight hours, make it an ideal location for fruit farming and winemaking. Farther afield to the east, in the Rocky Mountain foothills, large cattle ranches dot the landscape. The abundant variety of quality local foods coupled with a wealth of ethnic products from the province's multi-cultural population turns British Columbia into a cook's playground.

It was pure enjoyment travelling throughout British Columbia to research and update *Pacific Flavours*. I was impressed and delighted with the quality and expertise of the chefs. The standard of cuisine in Canada's most western province is exceptional and the recognition it receives internationally is truly deserved. I have profiled a sampling of dining establishments that take special interest in promoting cuisine that uses the best produce and products available in the region. The chefs have different talents, tastes and experiences and were enthusiastic about sharing them. I trust these selections, which range from formal gourmet fare to basic home cooking, will offer something for everyone. All the featured restaurants are licensed for liquor. Accommodations operated in conjunction with the restaurants are noted and described for easy reference.

In this second edition the Profile Section has been updated to include many new recommendations in the Okanagan Valley, Vancouver and its environs, Victoria and the Islands, Whistler Resort Area and the BC Rockies. Narrowing down restaurant selection is a challenging process, considering the wealth of fine dining establishments in the province. My choices were made through a combination of approaches: personal contact, information gathered from the print media, radio, television and the internet, as well as recommendations from colleagues in the food industry and trusted friends who love to eat well.

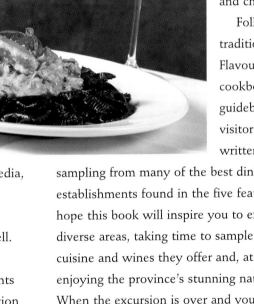

The recipe selection remains intact. Though many chefs have moved and some establishments have closed, the recipes chosen for the first edition continue to reflect the many cuisines of the region.

New to this edition are wine selections from Brent Hayman, Sommelier at Raincity Grill in Vancouver. He has matched each of the entrées to a BC-produced wine, applying his expert knowledge to make each of these recipes a truly gourmet experience. All of these wines are available from the winery, and most are also available from private stores, VQA vendors or BC liquor distribution outlets.

Preparing the book for publication was exciting, fun and, at times, challenging. Recipes were tested and adjusted for home use in my kitchen, with help from Shari Giffin, an excellent cook and good friend.

Pacific Flavours is an independent cookbook and guidebook, with no sponsorship or fees paid for inclusion. If you have questions regarding wheelchair-accessibility or dining and accommodation policies for children, contact the establishment in advance. The accompanying information is up-to-date at the time of publication, but it is important to keep in mind that occasionally restaurant and lodging ownership changes and chefs relocate.

Following the tradition of the Flavours Series cookbooks and guidebooks, I offer visitors and residents a written and pictorial sampling from many of the best dining establishments found in the five featured regions. I hope this book will inspire you to explore these diverse areas, taking time to sample the wonderful cuisine and wines they offer and, at the same time, enjoying the province's stunning natural beauty. When the excursion is over and you are once again immersed in life's daily routine, pick up this book and rekindle your memories. Prepare and enjoy a delicious meal using recipes from the featured restaurants, and after your satisfying meal, turn to the profiles section to start planning your next trip. Bon appetit!

— V.L.

MAPS

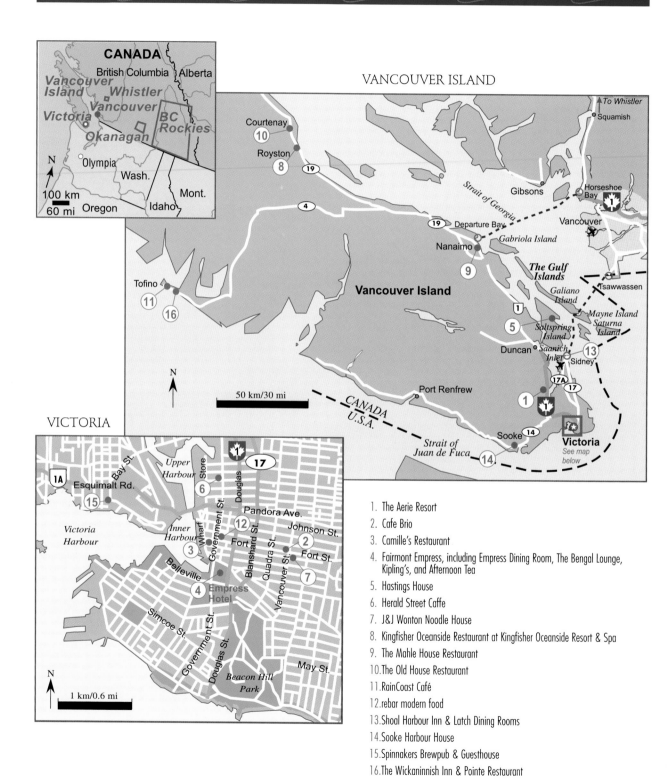

1. The Aerie Resort
2. Cafe Brio
3. Camille's Restaurant
4. Fairmont Empress, including Empress Dining Room, The Bengal Lounge, Kipling's, and Afternoon Tea
5. Hastings House
6. Herald Street Caffe
7. J&J Wonton Noodle House
8. Kingfisher Oceanside Restaurant at Kingfisher Oceanside Resort & Spa
9. The Mahle House Restaurant
10. The Old House Restaurant
11. RainCoast Café
12. rebar modern food
13. Shoal Harbour Inn & Latch Dining Rooms
14. Sooke Harbour House
15. Spinnakers Brewpub & Guesthouse
16. The Wickaninnish Inn & Pointe Restaurant

VANCOUVER & ENVIRONS

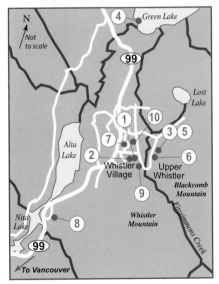

VANCOUVER DETAIL

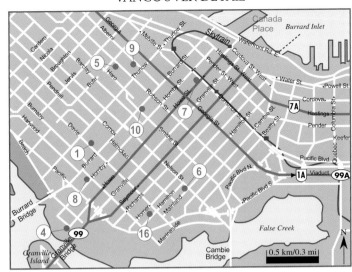

1. Bin 941 Tapas Parlour
2. Bin 942 Tapas Parlour
3. Bishop's Restaurant
4. C Restaurant
5. Cin Cin
6. Circolo
7. Diva at the Met
8. Il Giardino and Umberto's
9. Kirin Mandarin Restaurant
10. Le Crocodile
11. L'Emotion
12. Lumière Restaurant
13. Memphis Blues Barbecue House (2 locations)
14. Raincity Grill
15. Seasons Restaurant in Queen Elizabeth Park
16. Simply Thai
17. The Teahouse Restaurant in Stanley Park
18. Tojo's Restaurant

WHISTLER RESORT

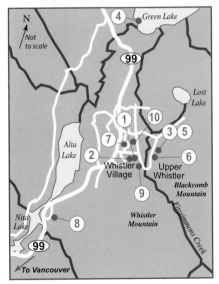

1. Araxi
2. Bearfoot Bistro
3. Chef Bernards Café
4. Edgewater Lodge
5. Fairmont Chateau Whistler including The Wildflower and Portbello
6. La Rua Restaurant
7. Quattro at Whistler
8. Rim Rock Café
9. Trattoria di Umberto Restaurant
10. Val D'Isere Restaurant

OKANAGAN VALLEY

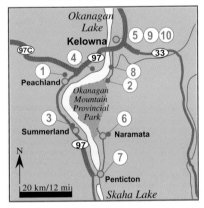

1. The Amphora Tapas Bar
2. Cedar Creek Estate Winery
3. Cellar Door Bistro and Catering
4. Old Vines Patio
5. Fresco Restaurant
6. Naramata Heritage inn and Spa
7. Salty's Beach House Restaurant
8. Sunset Veranda Restaurant at Summerhill Estate Winery
9. The Teahouse Restaurant at Kelowna Land and Orchard
10. The Williams Inn

BC ROCKIES & KOOTENAYS

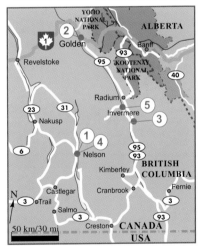

1. All Seasons Café
2. Eagle's Eye Restaurant at Kicking Horse Mountain Resort
3. Fairmont Hot Springs Resort
4. Fiddler's Green Restaurant
5. Strand's Old House Restaurant

APPETIZERS

THE PURPOSE OF THE APPETIZER IS TO TEASE ONE'S TASTE-BUDS, STIMULATING THE APPETITE FOR WHAT FOLLOWS... Without a doubt, the chefs who contributed to this chapter have remained true to that intent in these first-course recipes.

Included here are recipes for finger foods such as Tojo's Golden Roll from Tojo's Restaurant. Other recipes, such as Baked Artichokes with Garlic Mayonnaise from Cin Cin, are more suitable for formal sit-down dinners. Some of the recipes are even substantial enough to serve as light dinner or luncheon entrées.

In this section you will sample a wonderful variety of "taste tempters" that showcase the chefs' diverse culinary talents. Rare Ahi Tuna with Asian Papaya Slaw from Whistler's Rimrock Café highlights delicate Pacific tuna lightly seared to perfection, while Wild B.C. Sockeye Salmon on Red Shiso and Sesame Pancakes from Vancouver's Diva at the Met features paper-thin raw salmon at its succulent best.

Of course no Pacific Northwest cookbook would be worth its salt without recipes including fresh Dungeness crab and Pacific oysters. This celebrated West Coast fare is at its best in Nori-Wrapped Dungeness Crab Cakes with Lemongrass Cream from Oritalia, and in RainCoast Café's Fresh-Shucked Pacific Oysters with West Coast Splash.

I know that you will enjoy trying all of the offerings in this collection and that they will indeed tease your tastebuds.

◀ Grilled Fanny Bay Oysters with Smoked Paprika Mayonnaise

GRILLED FANNY BAY OYSTERS WITH SMOKED PAPRIKA MAYONNAISE

BEACH SIDE CAFÉ, WEST VANCOUVER, BC / *Executive Chef: Carol Chow*

Chef Chow's secret to serving perfect oysters is to make sure that they are not overcooked. Here, she highlights the delicate Fanny Bay oyster with a smoky Mediterranean paprika mayonnaise. Look for smoked sweet paprika in Mediterranean markets. For best results when making the mayonnaise, all the ingredients should be at room temperature.

8	cups water
1	onion, diced
1	leek, thinly sliced
1	lemon, halved
24	preshucked medium to large oysters
1	tbsp vegetable oil
	salt and pepper
	Smoked Paprika Mayonnaise (recipe follows)
	frisée* or other greens for garnish

In large saucepan, bring water, onion, leek and lemon to boil; reduce heat and simmer for 10 minutes. Remove from heat and strain into bowl. Return liquid to saucepan and bring to boil; add oysters, return to boil and immediately remove from heat.

Strain, reserving oyster stock for chowder or fish soup. Cool oysters under cold running water; shake to remove excess water. In bowl, lightly toss oysters with oil, and salt and pepper to taste. Heat grill over high heat; transfer oysters to grill and cook for 30 seconds. Turn and cook for another 30 seconds or until they are just cooked.

TO SERVE: Dollop mayonnaise in centre of each of 4 plates; arrange 6 oysters per plate in spoke-wheel fashion around mayonnaise. Garnish with frisée. *Serves 4.*

* A member of the chicory family, frisée has curly yellowish leaves.

Smoked Paprika Mayonnaise

1	egg yolk
2	tbsp white wine vinegar
1	tbsp Dijon mustard
	zest and juice of 1 lemon
1	shallot, minced
1	cup vegetable oil
1	tbsp smoked sweet paprika
dash	Tabasco Sauce
dash	Worcestershire sauce
	salt and pepper

In food processor, purée together egg yolk, vinegar, mustard, lemon zest and juice and shallot. With machine running, very gradually add oil until combined. Add paprika, Tabasco, Worcestershire sauce, and salt and pepper to taste: process for 30 seconds. Taste and adjust seasoning if necessary. Refrigerate until serving. *Makes 1 cup.*

FRESH-SHUCKED PACIFIC OYSTERS WITH WEST COAST SPLASH

RAINCOAST CAFÉ, TOFINO, BC / *Owner/Chef: Lisa Henderson*

Like a vintage wine, oysters develop a unique flavour, texture and size depending upon the environment in which they are raised. Of course, native British Columbians claim that the oyster cultivated at Fanny Bay on the eastern coast of Vancouver Island is simply the best. Oyster connoisseurs insist that fresh-shucked oysters on the half-shell are the only way to experience an oyster's true flavour. At RainCoast Café you can partake of that tradition with the café's own special West Coast Splash.

oysters to serve 4 to 6
West Coast Splash (recipe follows)

Discard any oysters that have damaged shells or that do not close when tapped. Brush with stiff brush under cold running water to remove dirt.

Wrap kitchen towel around your hand to protect it from sharp shell edges. Cup oyster in towel-wrapped hand; with other hand wedge tip of oyster knife into hinge of oyster, twisting until hinge separates. Sever muscle from top shell and remove shell. Gently run knife under oyster just to separate from shell. Set shucked oyster, in its shell, on bed of crushed ice on platter or on individual deep serving plates. Repeat with remaining oysters.

TO SERVE: Present shucked oysters on the shell. Accompany with bowl of West Coast Splash. *Serves 4 to 6.*

1	cup rice wine vinegar
1/3	cup liquid honey
2	tbsp sake (Japanese wine)
2	tbsp minced shallot
1/2	tsp freshly ground black pepper
1/2	tsp red pepper flakes
1/2	tsp salt
1/4	cup minced seeded English cucumber
1/4	cup minced daikon*
1/4	cup minced sweet red pepper
2	tbsp minced green onion
1 1/2	tbsp chopped fresh parsley
2	tsp black sesame seeds

West Coast Splash

In small saucepan over high heat, stir together vinegar, honey, sake, shallot, black pepper, red pepper flakes and salt; bring to boil and immediately remove from heat. Pour into bowl and let cool to room temperature. Cover and refrigerate until thoroughly chilled.

When chilled, stir in cucumber, daikon, red pepper, green onion, parsley and sesame seeds; cover and refrigerate until serving. *Makes 2 cups sauce.*

*Daikon is a large sweet Asian radish available in the produce section of most supermarkets and in Asian markets.

THAI CURRY BEEF WITH GINGER AÏOLI AND AVOCADO ON HEARTS OF ROMAINE

ORITALIA, VANCOUVER, BC / *Executive Chef: Julian Bond*

Chef Julian Bond has captured true Thai tradition with this appetizer of bold flavours and textures in perfect balance. The curry sauce is sweet and spicy, the aïoli is infused with hot red chili, and the romaine and burnoise of red pepper and cucumber are cold and crunchy. If you are left with extra curry sauce, serve it with grilled chicken or fish. Extra aïoli may be used with fish or cold cooked vegetables.

2	hearts romaine lettuce
1/2	cup finely diced sweet red pepper
1/2	cup finely diced peeled seeded cucumber
1	tsp vegetable oil
1	tsp butter
1	lb tenderloin premium, cut into 1/2-inch cubes
1	cup Curry Sauce (recipe follows)
	Ginger Aïoli (recipe follows)
1	avocado, peeled and diced

Wash romaine hearts and separate leaves; pat dry and set aside. In small bowl, combine red pepper and cucumber to make a burnoise; set aside.

In skillet, heat oil and butter over medium-high heat; briefly sear tenderloin cubes. Add Curry Sauce, stirring to combine. Remove from heat and keep warm.

TO SERVE: Arrange romaine leaves attractively on each of 4 or 6 large chilled plates. Drizzle centre of each leaf with Ginger Aïoli; top with diced avocado and beef. Garnish with burnoise of red pepper and cucumber. *Serves 4 to 6.*

1	tbsp vegetable oil
3/4	cup diced onion
1	tbsp red curry paste*
1	(15 oz/425 ml) can coconut milk
1/3	cup liquid honey
1	tbsp fish sauce*

Curry Sauce

For this recipe, make sure you purchase coconut milk and not cream of coconut which is used mainly for drinks and desserts. When you open the tin of coconut milk, you will find the cream at the top and the watery milk beneath.

In skillet, heat oil over medium heat; sauté onion and curry paste for 4 to 5 minutes or until onion is slightly softened. Add cream from top of coconut milk; cook, stirring often, for about 5 minutes or until mixture splits and caramelizes. Whisk in honey and remaining coconut milk; reduce by half. Stir in fish sauce and reduce slightly. *Makes 1 1/2 cups.*

*Look for red curry paste and fish sauce in the specialty section of most supermarkets and in Asian markets.

Ginger Aïoli

1	egg
1	egg yolk
2	tbsp minced gingerroot
1	tbsp minced garlic
1	tbsp sambal oelek*
3/4	cup peanut oil
3	tbsp lemon juice
1	tsp granulated sugar
1	tsp salt

In food processor, combine egg and egg yolk, gingerroot, garlic and sambal oelek; process until blended. With machine running, add half of the peanut oil in thin steady stream. When mixture begins to thicken, add lemon juice, sugar and salt; process until blended. With machine running, add remaining peanut oil, increasing the flow as mixture becomes pale. Cover and refrigerate until serving. *Makes 2 cups.*

Sambal oelek is a curry paste of chilies, brown sugar and salt found in Asian markets.

PAN-SEARED CAMEMBERT WITH SPICY CRANBERRY SAUCE

EDGEWATER LODGE, WHISTLER, BC / *Executive Chef: Thomas Piekarski*

Creamy Camembert literally oozes from its crunchy crust in this hors d'oeuvre, which is delicious spread on bread or crackers. As chef Piekarski does, accompany this appetizer with deep-fried parsley sprigs, assorted crackers, sliced rye bread or baguette and Spicy Cranberry Sauce.

1	egg
2	tsp water
1	wheel Camembert cheese*
1/4	cup all-purpose flour
1	cup bread crumbs
pinch	paprika
	salt and pepper
1/3	cup vegetable oil
1/3	cup butter
	fresh parsley sprigs
	Spicy Cranberry Sauce (recipe follows)

In bowl, beat egg with water. Dust Camembert with flour reserving excess; dip into egg wash, then roll in bread crumbs, pressing to adhere. Sprinkle cheese wheel with paprika, and salt and pepper to taste. (Can be wrapped in plastic wrap and refrigerated for up to 6 hours.)

In skillet or electric frying pan, heat oil and butter to medium-high; fry cheese wheel, turning once, for 5 to 7 minutes or until golden. Carefully remove and drain well on paper towel. Wash parsley, shake dry and dust with flour. Standing back to avoid splatters, drop into hot oil in same skillet. With tongs, quickly remove parsley and drain on paper towels.

TO SERVE: Place cheese wheel on serving plate; garnish with crunchy parsley sprigs. Serve with Spicy Cranberry Sauce. *Serves 4 to 8* depending on size of Camembert wheel.
Cheese wheels come in various sizes, the most common being 4 oz and 8 oz. You may also substitute Brie cheese.

12	oz fresh or frozen cranberries
1 1/4	cups granulated sugar
1	cup water
1/2	cup raisins
1/4	cup diced onion
2	tbsp vinegar
1	tbsp Worcestershire sauce
1/2	tsp salt
1/2	tsp Tabasco Sauce
1	tsp ground cumin

Spicy Cranberry Sauce (supplied by author)

This recipe makes more than required for the above recipe. You may halve the recipe or make the full amount and refrigerate or freeze the extra for another time.

In large glass bowl, combine cranberries, sugar, water, raisins, onion, vinegar, Worcestershire sauce, salt, Tabasco and cumin; microwave at high for 6 minutes. Stir and microwave for 2 minutes longer or until berries pop and sauce begins to thicken. Let cool. Pour into glass jars and refrigerate until serving. (Can be refrigerated for up to 2 weeks or frozen in plastic container for up to 6 months.) *Makes 4 cups.*

WILD B.C. SOCKEYE SALMON ON RED SHISO AND SESAME PANCAKES

DIVA AT THE MET, VANCOUVER, BC / *Executive Chef: Michael Noble*

If you have never tried raw fish before and are a little hesitant, then this is the appetizer to confidently begin your experience. The flavours and textures are wonderful and you realize that the thinly sliced fresh salmon is not only good, it is the essence of the dish.

1/2 lb frozen wild sockeye salmon
Red Shiso and Sesame Pancakes
(recipe follows)
mizuna greens* to serve 4
Miso Soy Dressing (recipe follows)

Thinly slice frozen salmon as for traditional Japanese sashimi (1/4 inch thick, making all cuts in same direction).

TO SERVE: Divide pancakes between 4 plates; top with mizuna greens. Arrange salmon pieces on top and drizzle Miso Soy Dressing around perimeter of plate. Serve at room temperature. *Serves 4.*

*Mizuna greens are feathery Japanese salad greens found in the specialty produce section of supermarkets. If mizuna is unavailable, substitute mesclun mix.

Red Shiso and Sesame Pancakes

1/2	cup all-purpose flour
1 1/2	tsp granulated sugar
3/4	tsp baking powder
1/4	tsp salt
5	red shiso leaves*, julienned
1	tbsp black sesame seeds
1	egg
1/2	cup milk
2	tbsp butter, melted

In bowl, combine flour, sugar, baking powder and salt; stir in shiso leaves and sesame seeds. Whisk together egg, milk and butter; pour over dry ingredients and stir just until thoroughly moistened. (Do not over mix.)

Heat lightly greased griddle to 375°F and spoon 4 dollar-size portions of batter onto griddle. Cook until bottom is golden and bubbles break on top but do not fill in; flip and cook for 1 minute longer or until lightly browned. *Makes 12 pancakes.*

Shisho leaves are from the perilla plant. Look for them in Japanese markets. If unavailable, substitute fresh basil.

Miso Soy Dressing

1/2	cup grapeseed oil
1/4	cup rice wine vinegar*
1 1/2	tbsp miso paste*
1	tbsp mirin* (Japanese rice wine)
1 1/2	tsp soy sauce
1	tsp sesame oil

In jar with tight-fitting lid, shake together grapeseed oil, vinegar, miso paste, mirin, soy sauce and sesame oil. Taste and adjust seasoning. *Makes 1 cup.*

Rice wine vinegar, mirin and miso paste are available in the specialty section of most supermarkets and in Asian markets.

NORI-WRAPPED DUNGENESS CRAB CAKES WITH LEMONGRASS CREAM

ORITALIA, VANCOUVER, BC / *Executive Chef: Julian Bond*

Sweet fresh Pacific Dungeness crab blends well with the slightly salty strips of sushi nori that wrap these delectable crab cakes. Add to this the unique lemon-ginger flavour of chef Julian Bond's Lemongrass Cream sauce and you have an appetizer or luncheon dish that will leave guests in awe. Garnish servings as desired with fresh herbs, edible flowers or enoki mushrooms.

1	lb Dungeness crabmeat
3	green onions, chopped
1	clove garlic, crushed
4	tbsp Habañero Mayonnaise (recipe follows)
1	tbsp granulated sugar
1	tbsp lime juice
1	tsp coarsely ground pepper
1	egg, lightly beaten (optional to moisten)
3	sheets sushi nori*
	egg wash (1 beaten egg + 1/2 tsp water)
1/2	cup all-purpose flour
2	cups bread crumbs
	vegetable oil
	Lemongrass Cream (recipe follows)

Clean and check crab for shell and cartilage: squeeze to remove excess liquid. In bowl, combine crab, green onions, garlic, Habañero Mayonnaise, sugar, lime juice, pepper, and enough egg to moisten (if desired). Using about 3 tbsp mixture per crab cake, form into circles. Cut sushi nori strips to width of circles and attach, moistening ends with some of the egg wash to seal. Coat open sides of circles with flour; dip in remaining egg wash, then bread crumbs.

In skillet, heat 1/2 inch oil over medium-high heat; fry crab cakes, turning once, for 5 to 7 minutes or until cooked through and light golden. Remove with slotted spatula and drain on paper towels.

TO SERVE: Creatively arrange crab cakes and Lemongrass Cream on individual dishes with garnish of choice. *Serves 4 to 6.*

Sheets of dried seaweed are available in the specialty section of some supermarkets and in Asian markets.

1	egg
1/4	cup olive oil
1	tbsp lime juice
1	tbsp finely diced seeded Habañero chili pepper
1/4	cup vegetable oil
	salt

Habañero Mayonnaise

Use this hot mayonnaise as a dressing for sandwiches or as a dipping sauce. It can be refrigerated for up to 4 days. Remember not to touch your eyes when handling Habañero chilies as they will burn. Wash hands after dicing. All ingredients should be at room temperature before combining.

In food processor, beat egg; with machine running, slowly add olive oil in thin steady stream. When mixture begins to thicken, blend in lime juice and Habañero chili pepper. With machine running, slowly add vegetable oil, increasing the flow as mayonnaise thickens and pales. Season with salt to taste. *Makes 3/4 cup.*

1	tsp vegetable oil
1/4	onion, diced
1/4	sweet yellow pepper, diced
1	clove garlic, minced
1/3	cup white wine
3	tbsp lemon juice
1	stalk lemongrass, cut in 2-inch lengths and crushed
1/4	cup crushed gingerroot
1	cup 35% cream
1/2	cup cooked mashed potato
1	tbsp liquid honey
	salt and white pepper

Lemongrass Cream

In saucepan, heat oil over medium-low heat; sweat onion, yellow pepper and garlic until vegetables are softened. Increase heat to medium; deglaze pan with wine and lemon juice. Enclose lemongrass and ginger in cheesecloth bag; add to sauce along with cream and potato. Reduce by half.

Remove cheesecloth bag, squeezing to extract juices. Add honey to sauce, season with salt and pepper to taste. In food processor, purée sauce; strain through fine-mesh sieve. *Makes 1 cup.*

RARE AHI TUNA WITH ASIAN PAPAYA SLAW

RIMROCK CAFÉ, WHISTLER, BC/ *Owner/Chef: Rolf Gunther*

The influence of other Pacific Rim countries is evident in Rolf Gunther's exquisitely prepared seared tuna on a fresh-tasting tropical papaya slaw.

1/2	lb Ahi tuna
1	tbsp extra-virgin olive oil
	salt and pepper
	cayenne pepper
1	ripe papaya, peeled and sliced
1/4	head sui choy, thinly sliced (or
1/4	head bok choy)
1	small red onion, thinly sliced
1	carrot, sliced into ribbons
	Lime Sesame Dressing (recipe follows)

Brush tuna with olive oil; season with salt, pepper and cayenne pepper to taste. Heat heavy-based skillet over high heat; sear tuna for 3 to 4 minutes per side or until rare.

In bowl, toss together papaya, sui choy, onion, carrot and enough of the dressing just to coat.

TO SERVE: Spoon slaw onto plates. Slice tuna very thinly and arrange decoratively over slaw. *Serves 4.*

1/4	cup soy sauce
1/4	cup mirin (Japanese rice wine)
2	tbsp lime juice
1 1/2	tsp minced gingerroot
1	green onion, sliced
1	tsp chopped fresh coriander
1	clove garlic, minced
1	tsp toasted sesame seeds*
1/2	tsp red pepper flakes
2	tbsp peanut oil
1	tsp sesame oil

Lime Sesame Dressing

In bowl combine soy sauce, mirin, lime juice, gingerroot, onion, coriander, garlic, sesame seeds and red pepper flakes; stir until combined. Gradually add peanut and sesame oils, whisking briskly until dressing is smooth. *Makes 3/4 cup.*

*To toast sesame seeds, heat skillet over low heat; cook sesame seeds, stirring constantly for 2 minutes or until golden.

BAKED ARTICHOKES WITH GARLIC MAYONNAISE

CIN CIN, VANCOUVER, BC / *Executive Chef: Romy Prasad*

When selecting artichokes choose ones that are heavy, with tightly closed leaves. Open leaves indicate that the flower bud is overripe.

4 to 6	large globe artichokes
	juice of 1 lemon
	water
8	tbsp + 1/4 tsp extra-virgin olive oil
1 3/4	cup thinly sliced onions
1 1/2	cup diced sweet red pepper
1 1/2	cup diced sweet green pepper
1 1/2	tbsp red wine vinegar
1	tbsp chopped fresh thyme (or 1 tsp dried)
2	bay leaves
2	cloves garlic, minced
	salt and pepper
1	cup soft bread crumbs
2	tbsp chopped fresh parsley
1/2	cup dry white wine
18 to 24	Kalamata olives
	Garlic Mayonnaise (recipe follows)

With a sharp knife remove outer leaves from artichokes. Break off stems and slice across bottoms to create a flat base. Grasp artichoke tops and cut off top two-thirds; discard tops. Holding artichoke bottoms in palm of hand, pull out central cone and remove the hairy choke.

Place artichokes in bowl and combine lemon juice with enough water to cover artichokes. This will prevent discolouration.

In skillet, heat 4 tbsp. of olive oil; add 1 cup onion, red and green peppers, vinegar, thyme, bay, garlic, salt and pepper. Sauté over medium heat until vegetables are softened, about 6 minutes; remove to 9" x 13" baking pan and reserve.

In same skillet, add 4 tbsp. olive oil, and 3/4 cup onion; sweat onion over medium-low heat until soft, about 6 to 8 minutes. Add breadcrumbs and parsley; stir to combine.

Dry artichokes and sprinkle with olive oil, salt and pepper to taste. Fill artichokes with bread crumb mixture; place upright on vegetable mixture in 9" x 13" oblong baking pan. Pour wine around artichokes. Cover with foil, sealing edges. Bake in 350°F oven for 1 1/4 hours.

TO SERVE: Place artichokes on each of 4 or 6 plates; spoon some of the vegetable mixture around artichokes. Pass olives and Garlic Mayonnaise alongside. *Serves 4 to 6.*

2	egg yolks
3	cloves garlic, crushed to paste
1	cup vegetable oil
1 1/2	tbsp warm water
1	tbsp white wine vinegar
3	tbsp extra-virgin olive oil

Garlic Mayonnaise

In food processor, process egg yolks and garlic until combined. With machine running, slowly add vegetable oil in thin steady stream. When mixture begins to thicken add water and vinegar; process until blended. With machine running, add olive oil and process until thickened. *Makes 1 1/2 cups.*

TOJO'S GOLDEN ROLL

TOJO'S RESTAURANT, VANCOUVER, BC / *Restaurateur: Hidekazu Tojo*

British Columbians of all ethnic backgrounds love the Asian influence in their cuisine, and sushi is a popular item with most residents. Sushi bars serving traditional first-course sashimi followed by a variety of sushi abound in Metro Vancouver. This special "golden roll" of sushi rice, fresh seafood and daikon sprouts is enclosed in a delicate thin egg crepe for excellent presentation and wonderful taste.

4	egg crepes (recipe follows)
	sushi rice (recipe follows)
1 1/2	tsp wasabi paste (Japanese horseradish)
2	tbsp mayonnaise
6	prawns, peeled, deveined and halved lengthwise
1/4	lb salmon, chopped
1/4	lb fresh crabmeat
1/4	lb scallops, chopped
1 1/2	cups daikon sprouts (or other fine sprouts of choice)
	flying fish roe (or fish roe of choice)
	gari (pickled ginger)

Place bamboo mat on work surface with long edge facing you. Place crepe golden side down on closest long edge of mat. Pat one-quarter of the rice over bottom half of the crepe leaving a half-inch space on the side and bottom edges. Spread thin band of wasabi across centre of rice. Arrange one-quarter of the prawns, salmon, crabmeat, scallops and daikon sprouts parallel to the wasabi. Spread thin band of mayonnaise parallel to the seafood.

Lift up the end of mat closest to you and using the mat as a guide, roll the crepe up firmly from the bottom, enclosing the crepe around the rice and seafood. Roll off the mat onto a cutting board and with a sharp knife cut roll crosswise into six equal pieces. Repeat with remaining crepes and filling.

TO SERVE: arrange sliced rolls on individual serving plates. Spoon flying fish roe on each slice and garnish with gari. *Serves 4 to 6.*

*Bamboo rolling mats are sold in Japanese specialty stores. If you can't find one, a folded tea towel is a good substitute.

3	eggs
	vegetable cooking spray

Egg Crepes

At Tojo's Restaurant the cooks make these crepes in a rectangular tamago-yaki pan. If you do not have one, increase the eggs to 4 and cook the crepes in an electric frypan. Cut the cooked crepes into 8 x 7 inch rectangles.

In bowl beat eggs lightly. Spray thin film of vegetable oil into pan. Heat tamago-yaki pan to medium or turn electric frypan to 300°F. Pour 1/4 of the beaten egg into pan and spread to form a thin crepe. Cook for one minute until light golden. Gently lift crepe from pan with spatula and lay on waxed paper to cool. Repeat with remaining egg. *Makes 4 crepes.*

1/4	cup rice vinegar
1	tbsp sugar
1/2	tsp salt
1	inch square piece of kelp
1 1/2	cups Japanese short-grain rice
2	cups cold water

Sushi Rice

In bowl, stir together vinegar, sugar and salt until sugar is dissolved. Add kelp; cover and refrigerate for at least 2 hours or for up to 12 hours.

Rinse rice until water runs clear. In saucepan, combine rice and water; bring to boil. Cover and reduce heat to very low; simmer for 15 minutes or until liquid is absorbed. Remove from heat and let stand 10 minutes. Transfer rice to shallow dish.

Remove kelp from vinegar mixture, discarding kelp. Pour liquid over warm rice and mix well. Let cool until no longer steaming. Cover with damp towel and cool until using. *Makes 4 cups.*

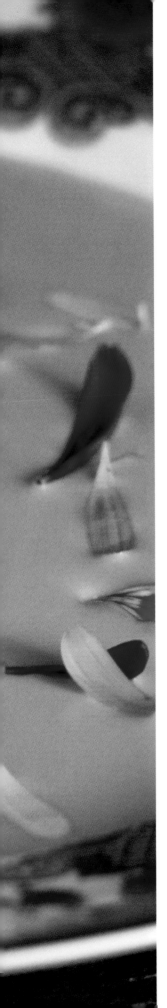

S O U P S

SOUPS ARE PERHAPS THE MOST VERSATILE AND SATISFYING
RECIPES IN A COOK'S REPERTOIRE.

When collecting these recipes I asked the chefs to share soups that
are representative of their establishment and locale. As a result, they
took full advantage of local seasonal produce and seafood. Their
contributions are exceptional and feature a variety of ingredients,
cuisines and cooking styles.

Chef Patt Dyck from The Country Squire offers us her Leek and
Fennel Soup and Sweet Red Pepper Soup — both of which highlight
fresh local produce. As an added bonus she shares her recipe for
Double-Strength Chicken Stock to ensure the richest soup possible.

On a warm summer day, serve chilled Sweet Pea Soup with Crème
Fraîche and Hand-Peeled Shrimp from North Vancouver's Beach Side
Café or Vichyssoise with Lobster Medallions from Le Crocodile. When
autumn rains begin to freeze into the snowflakes of winter, warm your
soul with Maureen Loucks' rich Smoked Gouda Soup from The Mahle
House Restaurant or RainCoast Café's Indonesian Sweet Potato,
Coconut and Peanut Soup.

The influence the Pacific Ocean has on British Columbia cuisine is
evident in the abundance of delicious soups and chowders featuring
seafood. For special occasions, start the menu with elegant Pacific
Oyster Stew from the kitchen of Pierre Delacote at Seasons Restaurant
in Queen Elizabeth Park or the subtle Lobster Bisque from The Empress
Room at The Fairmont Empress Hotel in Victoria.

◀ Leek and Fennel Soup

LOBSTER BISQUE

THE EMPRESS ROOM AT THE FAIRMONT EMPRESS HOTEL, VICTORIA, BC / *Executive Chef: David Hammonds*

Smooth and subtle best describes this delicious traditional bisque from the elegant Empress Room. Lobster bisque is an excellent secondary dish from a meal of fresh lobster. Simply save the shells for lobster stock and a small portion of the meat for garnish.

3	tbsp butter
1	stalk celery, sliced
1	carrot, sliced
1	large leek, chopped
1	onion, chopped
2	tbsp all-purpose flour
4 1/2	cups Lobster Stock (recipe follows)
1 1/4	cups 35% cream
	pinch cayenne pepper
	salt
1/2	cup lobster meat, cut in chunks

In heavy-based saucepan melt butter over medium heat; sauté celery, carrot, leek and onion, stirring gently, for 5 minutes. Whisk in flour and cook for 1 minute, stirring constantly. Whisk in stock until smooth; cook for about 20 minutes or until vegetables are tender.

In blender or food processor, purée soup in batches. Return to saucepan over medium heat; stir in cream, cayenne pepper and salt to taste. Stir in lobster meat. Garnish with fresh herbs or edible flower petals. Ladle into bowls. *Serves 4.*

	shells from 2 or 3 lobsters
6	cups water

Lobster Stock

You can cook the stock in advance and freeze for later use.

Crack or break up lobster shells into small pieces, being careful not to pulverize.

In large saucepan, combine lobster shells and water; bring to boil. Reduce heat to medium-low and simmer until reduced to 4 1/2 cups. Strain through fine-mesh sieve to remove all traces of shell. *Makes 4 1/2 cups.*

LEEK AND FENNEL SOUP

THE COUNTRY SQUIRE, NARAMATA, BC / *Owner/Chef: Patt Dyck*

The soups at The Country Squire have a special rich flavour because they contain chef Patt Dyck's own Double-Strength Chicken Stock. If you do not have the time or inclination to make stock, you may substitute any good-quality store-bought chicken stock, but be prepared to lose a little of the robust flavour.

3	tbsp olive oil
2	tbsp butter
2	medium leeks (white part only), chopped
2	fennel bulbs, trimmed and chopped
1/4	tsp salt
5	cups Double-Strength Chicken Stock
1	bouquet garni (parsley, bay leaf, thyme and rosemary tied in cheesecloth bag)
1/2	cup 35% cream
	salt and white pepper

In large, heavy-based saucepan, heat oil and butter over medium low heat; add leeks and fennel, stir well and sprinkle with salt. Cover and cook over low heat, stirring occasionally and being careful not to burn, for about 10 minutes or until softened.

Add chicken stock and bouquet garni; simmer, covered, for 30 minutes. Remove bouquet garni. In food processor, purée soup in batches. Strain and return to saucepan over low heat; pour in cream and simmer, stirring, until heated through. Season with salt and pepper to taste. Ladle into bowls. *Serves 4.*

DOUBLE-STRENGTH CHICKEN STOCK

THE COUNTRY SQUIRE, NARAMATA, BC / *Owner/Chef: Patt Dyck*

This recipe has two lists of ingredients as there is a second stage with a slight variation. If you take the time and effort to prepare this rich stock, you will be doubly pleased with the results of your soup.

Ingredients for Stage 1:

4	lb fresh chicken bones
20	cups cold water
2	stalks celery, sliced
2	carrots, sliced
1	onion, chopped
1	bouquet garni (parsley, thyme and bay leaves tied in cheesecloth bag)
1	tsp black peppercorns

Ingredients for Stage 2:

4	lb fresh chicken bones
10	cups cold water
10	cups chicken stock (from Stage 1)
2	stalks celery, sliced
2	carrots, sliced
1	onion, chopped
1	bouquet garni (see Stage 1)
1	tsp black peppercorns

Stage 1:

In stockpot cover bones with water; bring to boil. Reduce heat to low and simmer for 15 minutes, skimming off foam as it rises to surface until top is almost clear.

Stir in celery, carrots, onion, bouquet garni and peppercorns; reduce heat to low and simmer, without stirring, for 3 to 4 hours until liquid is reduced by half. Strain stock into large pot; refrigerate, uncovered, for 4 to 6 hours or until cold and fat is congealed on surfaces. Skim off and discard surface fat.

Stage 2:

Repeat method for Stage 1, using fresh bones and other ingredients listed for Stage 2. Strain double stock. Refrigerate, uncovered, for 4 to 6 hours or until fat is congealed on surface. Skim off fat and freeze in airtight container. Let thaw before using. *Makes 10 cups.*

SWEET RED PEPPER SOUP

THE COUNTRY SQUIRE, NARAMATA, BC / *Owner/Chef: Patt Dyck*

Count on this soup, which uses locally grown sweet red peppers, for a colourful presentation. Be careful not to spill — it stains.

5	tbsp butter
2	large onions, chopped
2	shallots, chopped
4	garlic cloves, crushed
6	sweet red peppers, seeds and membrane removed, chopped
1/2	tsp red pepper flakes
6	cups Double-Strength Chicken Stock* (recipe, page 30)
1 1/3	cups 35% cream
	salt and white pepper
	Tabasco Sauce (optional)
	Cucumber Garnish (recipe follows)

In large heavy-based saucepan, melt butter over medium heat; sauté onions, shallots and garlic, stirring often, for 5 to 8 minutes or until softened. Add red peppers and red pepper flakes to saucepan; cook, stirring, for 3 to 5 minutes. Pour in chicken stock, simmer for 30 minutes.

In food processor, purée soup in batches. Strain and return to saucepan over low heat. Stir in cream and simmer until heated through. Season with salt and pepper to taste. Add dash of Tabasco (if desired). Ladle into bowls; top each with heaping tablespoon of Cucumber Garnish. *Serves 6.*

1/2	English cucumber
1	tsp salt

Cucumber garnish

In food processor, chop cucumber finely. Pour into sieve set over bowl. Sprinkle with salt and let drain for 1 hour. Discard liquid. *Makes 1 1/2 cups.*

SWEET PEA SOUP WITH CRÈME FRAÎCHE AND HAND-PEELED SHRIMP

BEACH SIDE CAFÉ, WEST VANCOUVER, BC / *Executive Chef: Carol Chow*

This chilled soup is truly an all-season recipe. Use fresh peas from your garden or local market in the summer when they are abundant or substitute tender, quick-frozen peas from the supermarket at other times of the year.

2	tbsp butter
1	onion, diced
1	large leek (white part only), thinly sliced
3	cloves garlic, crushed
6	cups chicken stock
2	lb fresh or frozen green peas
	salt and white pepper
1/2	lb cooked shrimp, peeled and deveined
1	cup crème fraîche*

In large saucepan, heat butter over medium heat; sauté onion, leek and garlic for about 5 minutes or until onion is translucent. Add stock and peas; bring to boil. Reduce heat and simmer for 5 minutes or until peas are softened. Remove pan from heat and set in ice bath to cool quickly.

In food processor, purée soup in batches until smooth. Strain through sieve. Season with salt and pepper. Refrigerate until chilled.

Ladle into bowls; garnish with shrimp and dollop of crème fraîche. *Serves 4 to 6.*

*Crème fraîche, common to French cookery, is a thickened, smooth cream with a slight acrid, nutty flavour. In France the utilization of unpasteurized cream is common, but we in North America must use pasteurized cream, which lacks the bacteria needed for thickening. Traditional crème fraîche is sold in some specialty markets but is also easy to duplicate at home. In glass bowl, combine 1 cup 35% cream and 2 tbsp buttermilk. Cover and let stand at room temperature for 8 to 24 hours or until thickened. Stir and refrigerate for up to 10 days.

NOGGIN'S CHOWDER

SPINNAKERS BREWPUB & GUESTHOUSE, VICTORIA, BC / *Owner: Paul Hadfield*

Noggin's Chowder has long been a mainstay on the menu at Spinnakers Brewpub. Smooth, creamy, chock-full of seafood and with a hint of dill, it makes a complete meal when served with warm crusty bread. The joy of chowders is that you are not limited to specific seafood but may substitute any fresh fish or shellfish available.

1	clams
5	strips bacon, cut into 1-inch pieces
1	red onion, diced
2	carrots, diced
3	stalks celery, diced
4	cups fish stock
3	potatoes, peeled and cut into 1/2-inch cubes
4	sprigs fresh dill, chopped (or 2 tsp dried dillweed)
	salt and white pepper
1/2	lb scallops
1	lb halibut, cut into 1-inch cubes
1/4	lb smoked salmon, sliced into 1/4-inch strips
1 1/2	cups 10% cream
1	cup 35% cream
1	cup whole milk
2	tsp all-purpose flour
3/4	tsp vegetable oil

Scrub clams, discarding any that have broken shells or do not close when lightly tapped. In large saucepan, bring small amount of water to boil, steam clams for about 5 minutes or until they open. Drain; discard any that have not opened. Set clams aside.

In heavy-based saucepan or Dutch oven, fry bacon until crisp. Drain off excess fat. Add onion, carrots and celery to pan; cook over medium-low heat for 8 to 10 minutes or until softened. Add fish stock, potatoes, dill, and salt and pepper to taste; cover and simmer for 10 to 15 minutes or until vegetables are tender. Add halibut and scallops; cook just until fish turns opaque. Add smoked salmon, clams in shell, 10% cream, 35% cream and milk; heat gently without boiling. Blend flour with oil, whisk into chowder and simmer for 2 minutes or until slightly thickened. Taste and adjust seasoning with salt, pepper and dill if necessary. Ladle into bowls. *Serves 6 generously.*

CAYMAN ISLAND CHOWDER

SALTY'S BEACH HOUSE RESTAURANT, PENTICTON, BC / *Chef: Ken Large*

Chef Ken Large substitutes local Pacific Northwest seafood for the original Caribbean fare in this creation inspired from restaurant owner Rob Wylie's travels to the Cayman Islands. At Salty's the soup base is prepared in advance and fresh seafood is added for individual orders, ensuring that it is cooked to perfection. You may substitute fish and shellfish available to your area.

1	lb combination of Manila clams, mussels and B.C. pink swimming scallops in their shells
1/4	lb lean bacon, diced
1	onion, diced
2	stalks celery, diced
2	cloves garlic, crushed
6	cups water
1	can (28 oz) Italian plum tomatoes
1/2	cup ketchup
2	tbsp dry sherry
1 1/2	tbsp lemon juice
1	tbsp Thai fish sauce*
1	tbsp curry powder (or to taste)
1	tsp Worcestershire sauce
1/4	tsp Tabasco Sauce
1/2	lb salmon, cut in bite-size pieces
1/2	lb halibut, cut in bite-size pieces
1/2	lb shrimp, peeled and deveined

Scrub clams and mussels and remove beards from mussels. Discard any clams or mussels that do not close when tapped. Set aside.

In large heavy-based saucepan over medium heat, sauté bacon until it begins rendering fat. Add onion, celery, and garlic; sauté for 5 minutes or until vegetables are softened and bacon is crisp. Skim excess fat from saucepan if necessary. Add water, tomatoes, ketchup, sherry, lemon juice, fish sauce, curry powder, Worcestershire sauce and Tabasco to saucepan; taste and adjust seasoning. Bring to boil. Reduce heat and simmer for 30 minutes.

Add clams, mussels, scallops, salmon, halibut and shrimp; simmer for about 5 minutes or until fish is just cooked and clams and mussels open. (Discard any that have not opened.) Ladle into bowls. *Serves 6 to 8.*

*Look for Thai fish sauce in specialty sections of supermarkets or in Asian markets.

INDONESIAN SWEET POTATO, COCONUT AND PEANUT SOUP

RAINCOAST CAFÉ, TOFINO, BC / *Owner/Chef: Lisa Henderson*

The influence of Pacific Rim nations on British Columbia cuisine is evident in this sweet exotic Indonesian soup. Its aggressive yet complementary flavours makes it one of the most popular items on the menu. This recipe makes a large quantity. You may reduce it by half, but chef Wrigley suggests that you make the full amount to guarantee leftovers.

1	tbsp vegetable oil
1	large onion, chopped
6	cloves garlic, minced
2	shallots, minced
2	tbsp minced gingerroot
1 1/2	cups water
2 1/2	lb sweet potatoes, diced
1	tsp salt
1/2	tsp pepper
1/2	tsp red pepper flakes
1	cup creamy peanut butter (preferably organic)
1/4	cup tamari*
1	bunch fresh cilantro, chopped
2	cans 15 oz (425 g) coconut milk
	toasted coconut**
	chopped peanuts

In large saucepan, heat oil over medium heat; sauté onion, garlic, shallots and gingerroot, stirring often, for 5 minutes or until softened. Add water, sweet potatoes, salt, pepper and red pepper flakes; bring to boil. Reduce heat to low; cover and simmer potatoes for 20 to 30 minutes or until tender.

Stir in peanut butter, tamari and cilantro. In food processor, purée in batches, pouring in enough of the coconut milk to reach desired consistency.

Return to saucepan and reheat gently; taste and adjust seasoning if necessary. Ladle into bowls; garnish with toasted coconut and chopped peanuts. *Serves 8 to 10.*

*Tamari is a sauce made from soybeans that is similar to soy sauce but thicker and with a distinct mellow flavour. Look for it in the specialty section of supermarkets or in Asian markets.

**To toast coconut, spread on baking sheet and bake in 350ºF oven, stirring often and being careful to prevent burning, for 10 to 12 minutes or until golden.

CREAM OF CHANTERELLE SOUP WITH BLUEBERRY CRÈME FRAÎCHE

RIMROCK CAFÉ, WHISTLER, BC / *Owner/Chef: Rolf Gunther*

When the lovely trumpet-shaped chanterelle mushroom is in season, Rolf Gunther uses it in this delicately flavoured soup. If unavailable, substitute other mushrooms of choice.

3	tbsp butter
1/2	lb fresh chanterelle mushrooms, chopped
2	shallots, minced
2	cloves garlic, minced
3/4	cup finely diced carrot and celery
1/3	cup dry white wine
1 1/2	cups 35% cream
3	cups vegetable stock (or chicken stock)
	salt and pepper
	Blueberry Crème Fraîche (recipe follows)
2 to 3	oz smoked trout, thinly sliced

In saucepan, melt butter over medium heat; sauté mushrooms, shallots, garlic, carrot and celery until vegetables are softened. Deglaze pan with wine. Stir in cream and cook, stirring often, until reduced by half. Stir in vegetable stock; season with salt and pepper to taste. Simmer for about 10 minutes or until flavours are blended.

In food processor, purée soup in batches until smooth. Taste and adjust seasoning. Return to saucepan and reheat gently. Ladle into bowls; garnish with dollop of Blueberry Crème Fraîche and smoked trout slices. *Serves 4.*

1/2	cup crème fraîche*
2	tbsp blueberries, puréed

Blueberry Crème Fraîche

Blend together crème fraîche and blueberries until smooth and creamy. *Makes 1/2 cup.*

*If unable to find fresh crème fraîche, make this inexpensive version at home. In glass container combine 1/2 cup 35% cream and 1 tbsp buttermilk. Cover and let stand at room temperature for 12 to 24 hours or until thickened. Stir and refrigerate until ready to use.

HOT-AND-SOUR SOUP

SPINNAKERS BREWPUB & GUESTHOUSE, VICTORIA, BC / *Sous Chef: Dicky Lum*

This variation of a traditional Asian hot-and-sour soup was created by Dicky Lum and features Spinnakers own malt vinegar. Enjoy its tart, tangy, sweet-and-sour flavour.

6	cups beef stock
1/2	cup thinly sliced mushrooms
6	tbsp malt vinegar
1	large tomato, peeled, seeded and slivered
1	tbsp tomato paste
1	tbsp sesame oil
1	tsp brown sugar
1	tsp soy sauce
1/2	tsp Asian chili paste
2	tbsp cornstarch
2	tbsp water
1/2	cup water chestnuts, thinly sliced
2	green onions, cut in 3-inch lengths and slivered
	salt and pepper

In large saucepan, stir together stock, mushrooms, vinegar, tomato, tomato paste, sesame oil, brown sugar, soy sauce and chili sauce; bring to boil. Reduce heat and simmer, stirring occasionally, for 15 minutes. In small bowl, combine cornstarch and water; add to soup and cook, stirring until slightly thickened.

Just before serving, add water chestnuts, and two-thirds of the green onions; season with salt and pepper to taste. Ladle into bowls; garnish with remaining green onions. *Serves 4.*

VICHYSSOISE WITH LOBSTER MEDALLIONS

LE CROCODILE, VANCOUVER, BC / *Owner/Chef: Michel Jacob*

Chef Michel Jacob prepares this very delicate, smooth chilled soup in the traditional French manner but with an addition of lobster medallions and garnish of tobiko eggs and fresh herbs.

2	tbsp butter
1	medium onion, diced
1	medium leek, chopped
1	lb Yukon gold potatoes, peeled and diced
1	clove garlic, minced
1	bouquet garni (parsley, thyme and bay leaves tied in cheesecloth bag)
2	cups vegetable stock (or chicken stock)
1/2	cup 35% cream
1/4	cup spinach mousse*
1	whole lobster tail, poached
2	tsp tobiko eggs
2	tsp each chopped fresh chives and parsley

In large saucepan, heat butter over medium heat; sauté onion for 5 minutes or until softened. Add leek, potatoes, garlic and bouquet garni; pour in vegetable stock. Cover and simmer for 1 hour. Remove bouquet garni and simmer for 30 minutes longer.

In food processor, purée soup in batches. If necessary strain through sieve to remove stringy portions. Cover and refrigerate until chilled.

Just before serving, stir in cream and spinach mousse. Slice lobster tail crosswise and add to soup. Ladle into bowls; garnish with tobiko eggs, parsley and chives. *Serves 4.*

*Le Crocodile uses a spinach mousse in this recipe but you can substitute 1/4 cup cooked spinach that has been puréed and passed through a sieve.

SMOKED GOUDA SOUP

THE MAHLE HOUSE RESTAURANT, NANAIMO, BC / *Owner/Chef: Maureen Loucks*

Warm up on winter days with this rich, smoky cheese soup. It would also work well as a cheese fondue served with crusty French bread cubes; simply reduce a little longer during the simmering stage.

1/4	cup butter
1	large onion, chopped
2	tsp minced garlic
1	tbsp all-purpose flour
6	cups chicken stock
	salt and white pepper
2	cups 35% cream
8	oz shredded smoked Gouda cheese
	chopped fresh chives or basil

In saucepan, melt butter over medium-low heat; sweat onion until translucent. Add garlic and cook, stirring often, for 2 minutes. Whisk in flour; cook, stirring constantly, for 1 minute. Stir in chicken stock and season with salt and pepper to taste; bring to boil. Reduce heat and simmer, stirring frequently, for 30 to 45 minutes. Stir in cream and cook, stirring often, until reduced slightly. Stir in cheese until melted and smooth.

In food processor, purée soup in batches. Strain and return to saucepan; reheat gently. Ladle into bowls; garnish with chives or basil. *Serves 6.*

CARROT AND SAGE VELOUTÉ

THE AERIE RESORT, MALAHAT, BC / *Chef de Cuisine: Chris Jones, Sous-Chef: Christophe Letard*

Caramelized carrots give this soup its warm golden colour and rich flavour. Accompanied by fresh biscuits or warm crusty rolls, it is the ideal meal-in-a-bowl for the chilling days of autumn and winter.

1 1/2	lb carrots, sliced
2	tbsp olive oil
1	onion, diced
6	cloves garlic, minced
3	stalks celery, diced
1	bay leaf
5	whole peppercorns
2	cups Riesling
3 to 4	cups chicken stock
1/4	cup arborio rice
1	tbsp chopped fresh sage (or 1 tsp dried)
	10% cream (optional)
	fresh sage sprigs

In bowl, toss carrots with half of the oil; transfer to roasting pan and bake in 350°F oven for about 45 minutes or until tender and caramelized. In large heavy-based saucepan, heat remaining oil over medium heat; sauté onion, garlic, celery, bay leaf and peppercorns until onions are softened and smell sweet. Add wine and cook, stirring often, until reduced by two-thirds.

Add roasted carrots, chicken stock, rice and chopped sage to pan; bring to boil. Reduce heat and simmer, stirring occasionally, for 25 minutes. Remove bay leaf.

In food processor, purée soup in batches. Pass through sieve. Reheat gently, adding additional stock or 10% cream if necessary to reach desired consistency. Ladle into bowls and sprinkle with sage sprigs. *Serves 6.*

PACIFIC OYSTER STEW

SEASONS RESTAURANT IN QUEEN ELIZABETH PARK, VANCOUVER, BC / *Executive Chef: Pierre Delacote*

There are some who claim that the oyster is an aphrodisiac, but don't let that be the only reason to savour this delicate but rich soup. Its elegant presentation also makes a stunning first course when entertaining. If you are unable to find local Fanny Bay oysters, substitute fresh oysters of your choice.

1/4	cup unsalted butter
1	medium leek (white part only), julienned
1/4	cup dry white wine
1 2/3	cups 35% cream
20	fresh-shucked Fanny Bay oysters with juice
	salt
	freshly cracked black pepper

In shallow skillet, heat butter over medium heat; sauté leek, stirring for about 20 seconds, being careful not to brown. With slotted spoon, remove leek and set aside on plate. Deglaze skillet with wine. Add cream and oysters with juice; bring to rolling boil. With slotted spoon, remove oysters and divide equally among 4 very hot soup plates. Return sauce to boil; reduce for a few seconds and season with salt to taste. Ladle sauce over oysters; top with leeks and finish with freshly cracked black pepper. *Serves 4.*

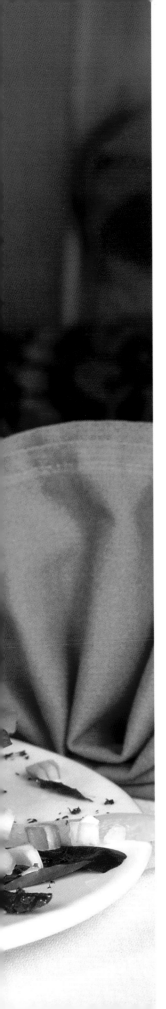

SALADS

IN TODAY'S WORLD, THE TERM "SALAD" CAN MEAN ANYTHING FROM A MIX OF SIMPLE GREENS DRIZZLED WITH A BASIC vinaigrette to an elaborate main-course dish that includes all food groups. The choice is yours to dress up or down according to your inclination.

The contributing chefs have provided a wide variety of recipes featuring the joining of their culinary backgrounds with the local produce of the region. You are guaranteed to find a number of recipes to add to your permanent collection in these ingenious offerings.

Many of the recipes, such as Sunomono Salad from The Grotto Restaurant in Nanaimo, demonstrate the strong Asian influence in West Coast cuisine. There are a number of interesting warm salads, including Cellar Door Bistro's Cellar Door Caesar, a unique variation on the traditional Caesar salad.

When fresh garden beans are in season, try The Amphora Bistro's Green and Yellow Bean Salad with Warm Bacon Vinaigrette, which showcases fresh Okanagan Valley produce.

Salads provide an ideal opportunity to promote healthier eating. Use olive and canola oils, which are the highest in monounsaturated fats of all oils, and when possible, serve dressings on the side to allow individuals to add only the desired amount.

◀ Edgewater Salad

EDGEWATER SALAD

EDGEWATER LODGE, WHISTLER, BC / *Executive Chef: Thomas Piekarski*

Chef Piekarski, who garnishes his house salad of organic greens and vegetables with edible flowers, describes it as "a visually pleasing array of seasonal greens and tomatoes, enlivened by a simple lemon, herb, garlic and olive oil dressing." The variety of garden vegetables in this recipe is extensive; you may want to substitute greens of choice if any are unavailable.

	salad greens and vegetables to serve 4 to 6 (e.g. sorrel, pea tips, arugula, ruby chard, kale, mizuna, fava tips)
2	green onions, sliced
1/2	sweet red pepper, julienned
1/2	sweet green pepper, julienned
1/2	sweet yellow pepper, julienned
1	large or 2 small tomatoes, cut in wedges
1/4	cup chopped fresh parsley
	Balsamic Sesame Vinaigrette (recipe follows)
	garnish of edible flowers (e.g. pansies, rose petals, violets, daisies, geraniums, marigolds, nasturtiums)*

In large bowl, combine salad greens and vegetables, green onions, red, green and yellow peppers, tomatoes and parsley; toss with Balsamic Sesame Vinaigrette just to coat. Arrange salad on chilled salad plates and garnish with edible flowers. *Serves 4 to 6.*

*use only flowers that are pesticide free.

Balsamic Sesame Vinaigrette

1/2	cup balsamic vinegar
2	tbsp brown sugar
1/4	cup olive oil
1/4	cup sesame oil
1	large clove garlic, minced
1	tbsp lemon juice
	salt and pepper
1/2	cup vegetable oil

In blender, mix balsamic vinegar and brown sugar for 1 minute. With blender running, add olive and sesame oils in slow steady stream, blending until smooth. Mix in garlic, lemon juice, and salt and pepper to taste. With blender running, add vegetable oil in slow steady stream, blending until bonded and silky. *Makes 1 1/2 cups.*

GREEN AND YELLOW BEAN SALAD WITH A WARM BACON VINAIGRETTE

THE AMPHORA TAPAS BAR AT HAINLE VINEYARDS ESTATE WINERY, PEACHLAND, BC

This decidedly different salad features Okanagan Valley produce. The string beans, cubed potatoes and delicious apple cider and mustard vinaigrette make a hearty salad that can readily be served as a luncheon entrée.

1	lb Blue Lake or other green beans, trimmed
3/4	lb yellow wax beans, trimmed
1/2	cup fresh chives, cut in 2-inch lengths
1/4	cup coarsely chopped Italian parsley
1/4	cup coarsely chopped celery leaves
1/2	lb bacon, diced
1	cup Yellow Finn or German Fingerling or other yellow fleshed potatoes, peeled and cut into 1/4-inch cubes
1/2	cup thinly sliced shallots
4	cloves garlic, minced
1/4	cup grainy Dijon mustard
1/3	cup organic apple cider (hard or soft)
1/3	cup organic apple cider vinegar
1/2	cup olive oil
	salt and pepper
2	cups coarsely chopped yellow tomatoes (optional)

In pot of boiling salted water blanch green and yellow beans for about 3 to 4 minutes or until al dente. Plunge beans immediately into cold water to stop cooking; drain and place in large serving bowl. Add chives, parsley and celery leaves; stir to combine. Set aside.

In heavy skillet, cook bacon over medium heat until crisp. With slotted spoon, transfer to paper towel to drain. Drain all but 3 tbsp fat from skillet. Return skillet to medium-high heat; cook potatoes for 2 to 3 minutes or until starting to brown. Add shallots; cook, stirring often, for 2 to 3 minutes or until lightly browned. Add garlic; cook, stirring often, for 1 to 2 minutes.

Stir in mustard; cook, stirring, for a few minutes or until moisture is almost evaporated. Pour in cider and cider vinegar and increase heat to high; cook until volume is reduced by half. Stir in bacon. Remove from heat; lightly whisk in olive oil until well blended. Season with salt and pepper to taste.

While dressing is still warm, pour over vegetable mixture; toss to combine. Let stand for 15 minutes before serving. Add tomatoes (if using) just before serving. *Serves 6 to 8.*

SPINNAKERS MIXED GREENS WITH RASPBERRY VINAIGRETTE

SPINNAKERS BREWPUB & GUESTHOUSE, VICTORIA, BC / *Owner: Paul Hadfield*

Spinnakers likes to highlight products made on the premises. This rosy, semisweet vinaigrette features the restaurant's special malt vinegar, which may be purchased on site. You can substitute malt vinegar of your choice.

1	lb mixed salad greens
	Raspberry Vinaigrette (recipe follows)

Arrange salad loosely on plates and drizzle with Raspberry Vinaigrette. *Serves 4.*

Raspberry Vinaigrette

2	cups water
2/3	cup fresh raspberries
1/4	cup granulated sugar
1/4	cups chopped fresh basil
2	tbsp malt vinegar
1 1/2	tbsp Dijon mustard
1	clove garlic, crushed
1	cup olive oil
	salt and pepper

In small saucepan, combine water, raspberries, sugar and basil; bring to boil. Cook, stirring, until reduced by half. Pass through sieve into bowl to remove seeds. Let cool.

In blender, purée raspberry juice, vinegar, mustard and garlic. With machine running, add oil in slow steady stream, blending until emulsified. Season with salt and pepper to taste. *Makes 1 1/2 cups.*

SPICY MESCLUN WITH AVOCADO, MANGO AND STILTON CHEESE

THE LATCH COUNTRY INN, SIDNEY, BC / *Owner/Chef: Heidi Rust*

Mesclun is a mix of young salad greens and is sold in the specialty section of most produce departments. The mix may vary but will commonly include arugula, oak leaf, radicchio, sorrel, frisée and dandelion. Chef Heidi Rust suggests that for a slight variation of flavour you can also use feta or goat cheese instead of the Stilton.

mesclun mix to serve 6

1 avocado, peeled and thinly sliced

1 ripe mango, peeled and thinly sliced

4 oz Stilton cheese, crumbled

Balsamic Vinaigrette (recipe follows)

Wash and thoroughly dry mesclun. Arrange attractively on 6 large plates; top with avocado and mango slices. Sprinkle with Stilton; drizzle with Balsamic Vinaigrette. *Serves 6.*

1/4 cup balsamic vinegar

2 tbsp chopped fresh basil

1 tbsp Dijon mustard

1 large clove garlic, minced

1 tsp grated gingerroot

1 cup olive oil

salt and pepper

Balsamic Vinaigrette

Whisk together vinegar, basil, mustard, garlic and ginger. In slow steady stream, whisk in olive oil until emulsified. Season with salt and pepper to taste. *Makes 1 1/3 cups.*

CAPRESE SALAD OF TOMATOES AND BOCCONCINI

BORGO ANTICO RISTORANTE, VANCOUVER, BC / *Owner: Umberto Menghi*

Not only does this salad taste very Italian, it also takes on the colours of Italy. Like the stripes of the national flag, ripe red Roma tomatoes, creamy white bocconcini cheese and green basil combine for an Italian-style experience.

1/2	cup balsamic vinegar
	pinch granulated sugar
4	Roma tomatoes, sliced
	salt and pepper
4	balls buffalo bocconcini* sliced
	finely chopped fresh basil leaves
4	tbsp extra-virgin olive oil

In saucepan over medium heat, stir vinegar with sugar; cook, stirring often, until reduced by one-quarter. Set aside and let cool.

TO SERVE: On each of 4 salad plates, arrange tomato slices in circle; season lightly with salt and pepper. Top with bocconcini slices; garnish with fresh basil leaves. Drizzle balsamic reduction around perimeter of plates and olive oil on top of bocconcini. *Serves 4.*

*Bocconcini are small balls of fresh mozzarella that are usually packed in water or whey. Use regular cow's milk bocconcini if buffalo are not available.

CAMBOZOLA CALDO CON CROSTINI

TRATTORIA DI UMBERTO RESTAURANT, WHISTLER, BC / *Owner: Umberto Menghi*

Crostini means "little toasts" in Italian, and this version, topped with tomato and roasted garlic, makes a wonderful accompaniment to a salad of lightly dressed greens and hot Cambozola cheese. The Rockies may surround the restaurant but the aroma is pure Alps!

8	slices French stick (baguette), sliced on diagonal 3/8 inch thick
4	tomatoes
6	cloves roasted garlic, minced
	mixed greens to serve 6
2	oz Cambozola cheese, sliced 1/2 inch thick
1	tbsp extra-virgin olive oil
1	tbsp balsamic vinegar

Toast bread in 375°F oven until lightly browned; set aside.

Slice tomatoes in half. Hold each half in palm of hand, extract juices and seeds; dice. In bowl, combine diced tomato and garlic; spread on toasted bread. Set aside.

Place sliced Cambozola on baking sheet and broil for about 1 minute or until browned.

Meanwhile, in bowl, whisk together olive oil and balsamic vinegar. Add greens and toss to coat.

TO SERVE: Arrange greens in the centre of large platter. Arrange crostini around outside of platter. Top with Cambozola. May also be served on individual salad plates as seen in photo. *Serves 4.*

SUNOMONO SALAD

THE GROTTO, NANAIMO, BC / *Owner: Mike Yoshida, Chef: Dave Armour*

Chef Dave Armour suggests serving this refreshing salad as a first course or luncheon entrée on a hot summer's day. For a variation, you can substitute 1/4 lb Dungeness crab for the shrimp.

4	oz dried yam noodles*
	vegetable oil
	Boston or Bibb lettuce to serve 4
1/2	cucumber, peeled, seeded and julienned
1	Granny Smith apple, cored, peeled and sliced
1/2	lb cooked shrimp, peeled and deveined
1/2	tsp lemon juice
	Sunomono Dressing (recipe follows)

In pot of boiling water cook noodles for 2 to 4 minutes or until al dente; drain and rinse under cold running water. Transfer noodles to bowl; toss with small amount of vegetable oil to keep from sticking. Cover and refrigerate until chilled.

In large bowl, combine noodles, lettuce, cucumber, apple and shrimp; toss with lemon juice. Lightly coat salad with Sunomono Dressing; toss and serve on chilled salad plates. *Serves 4.*

*Asian noodles are made from a variety of sources: wheat, rice, soy, yam, etc. If unable to find yam noodles, substitute 1 1/2 pkg ramen noodles.

1/4	cup mirin (Japanese rice wine)
1	tbsp granulated sugar
2	tsp soy sauce
1	tsp grated gingerroot
1	tsp lemon juice

Sunomono Dressing

In small bowl, whisk together mirin, sugar, soy sauce, gingerroot and lemon juice until sugar is dissolved. *Makes 1/3 cup.*

CELLAR DOOR CAESAR

CELLAR DOOR BISTRO & CATERING, SUMMERLAND, BC / *Chef: Dana Reinhardt*

How delightfully different — Caesar salad with grilled romaine lettuce! The presentation is unique and the taste is exceptional.

1	tbsp grainy Dijon mustard
1 1/2	tsp minced garlic
1	tsp Thai fish sauce*
1/2	tsp pepper, freshly ground
1/4	tsp Worcestershire sauce
1	cold egg yolk
3/4	cup vegetable oil
2 1/2	tbsp lemon juice
2	heads romaine lettuce, outer leaves removed
1/2	cup shredded Asiago cheese
	Herbed Croutons (recipe follows)

In food processor, combine mustard, garlic, fish sauce, pepper, Worcestershire sauce and egg yolk; purée until smooth. With machine running, add oil in slow steady stream, processing until thickened. Add lemon juice; pulse to combine. Cover and set aside in refrigerator.

Heat grill to 400° to 450°F. Cut romaine into quarters if large and into thirds if small. Spray both sides with light coating of vegetable oil and place on hot grill; char leaves slightly on both sides. To serve: Arrange on large dinner plates. Drizzle dressing along length of romaine; top with Asiago cheese and Herbed Croutons. *Serves 6 to 8.*

*Thai fish sauce is sold in the specialty section of most supermarkets.

Herbed Croutons

1/2	loaf good-quality peasant bread
1 to 2	tbsp vegetable oil
1/2	tsp minced garlic
1	tbsp chopped fresh herbs (basil, chives, thyme)
1	tbsp butter, melted
	sea salt and pepper

Cut bread into 1-inch cubes. Heat skillet over medium heat and coat bottom of pan with oil; cook bread cubes for 4 to 5 minutes, turning to brown on all sides. Add garlic, herbs and melted butter; toss with croutons to coat. Season with salt and pepper to taste. *Makes 4 to 5 cups croutons.*

SPINACH SALAD WITH HONEY DRESSING AND PANCETTA FETA TUQUES

LA RUA RESTAURANTE, WHISTLER, BC / *Executive Chef: Tim Muehlbauer*

Chef Tim Muehlbauer creates a new twist on the traditional spinach salad. The honey dressing is sweet but not overpowering, and his broiled Italian bacon and goat cheese "hat" tops off the salad in an unique way.

4	slices pancetta*
3 oz	feta cheese, crumbled
1 lb	fresh spinach, trimmed and torn
	Honey Dressing (recipe follows)
8	cultivated white mushroom caps, sliced
1	small bunch fresh parsley, chopped
2	hard-cooked eggs, finely chopped

Place slices of pancetta on baking sheet; sprinkle with feta. Set aside.

In large salad bowl, toss spinach with small amount of Honey Dressing to moisten. Add mushrooms and half of the chopped parsley; toss.

Broil pancetta "tuques" under broiler until golden, being careful to watch that cheese does not burn.

TO SERVE: Arrange spinach in centre of serving dishes; drizzle with remaining honey dressing if desired. Garnish with egg and remaining parsley; top with panchetta "tuque." *Serves 4.*

Pancetta (cured Italian bacon) is available in the deli section of most supermarkets or Italian grocery stores.

1	cup white wine
1/3	cup minced shallots
1/3	cup liquid honey
4	tsp raspberry vinegar
1	tsp Dijon mustard
1	tsp lemon juice
	pinch ground cardamom
4	tbsp vegetable oil (or flavoured oil of choice)

Honey Dressing

In small saucepan over medium-high heat, cook wine and shallots for 12 to 15 minutes or until reduced to syrupy consistency.

In bowl, whisk together wine mixture, honey, vinegar, Dijon mustard, lemon juice and cardamom. Gradually whisk in oil until emulsified. *Makes 1 cup.*

ENTRÉES

THERE ARE SO MANY MEATS TO CHOOSE FROM AND SO MANY WAYS TO PREPARE THEM, I FOUND MYSELF WONDERING HOW I could possibly narrow the selection for a well-rounded cookbook. I decided the best course of action was simply to ask the chefs to contribute their favourite meat entrées. Presto! The solution of what to include was in their replies.

In this section you will find a superb variety of recipes encompassing beef, pork, chicken, game, veal and lamb. All the recipes are innovative and represent the best of local ingredients. Edgewater Marinated Venison Medallions from chef Thomas Piekarski in Whistler and Chanterelle-Stuffed Venison Medallions from The Herald St. Caffe in Victoria feature farm-raised venison that melts in your mouth. Chicken is prepared in a variety of ways, including a curry, a coq-au-vin and breasts stuffed with smoked salmon. Two of the chefs showed their partiality for pork and responded with recipes for pork tenderloin with fruit and ribs Asian-style.

Whether you are a novice or a seasoned cook, you will find numerous recipes in this section suited to your range of expertise. Many are ideal for family-style meals while others are perfect for entertaining.

◀ Cinnamon Chili Rub Flank Steak

CINNAMON CHILI RUB FLANK STEAK

BIN 941 TAPAS PARLOUR, VANCOUVER, BC / *Owner/Chef: Gord Martin*

Do not be overwhelmed by the combination of ingredients in this Pacific Northwest adaptation of a southern Texan dish. The result is simply delicious. At BIN 941 this "tapatiser" is served with black pepper pommes frites but the chef says you can also accompany the dish with whipped mashed potatoes or rice and fresh seasonal vegetables. Chef Martin cautions that you should cook flank steak only to rare as overcooking toughens it.

1/3	cup chili powder
2	tbsp cinnamon
	pinch salt
	pepper
2	lb flank steak
1 to 2	tsp olive oil
1/2	cup beef stock
1/4	cup liquid honey
1	tbsp canned chipotle pepper, puréed
1	tbsp unsalted butter

In bowl, combine chili powder, cinnamon, salt and generous amount of pepper. Trim steak and lightly score in a crosshatch fashion on both sides. Rub chili mixture into steak; place in large resealable plastic bag and marinate in refrigerator for at least 2 hours or for up to preferred 24 hours.

In skillet, heat oil over high heat; sear steaks for about 3 minutes per side just until rare. Transfer to plate and let stand. Return skillet to high heat; deglaze pan with stock. Add honey and chipotle pepper; reduce, stirring often, until thickened. Whisk butter into sauce; remove from heat and strain.

TO SERVE: Thinly slice steak across the grain and drizzle with sauce. *Serves 4 to 6.*

Wine suggestion — 2001 Sandhill Cabernet Franc

SMOKED PORK TENDERLOIN WITH OVEN-DRIED DAMSON PLUMS

CELLAR DOOR BISTRO & CATERING, SUMMERLAND, BC / *Chef: Dana Reinhardt*

At the Cellar Door Bistro, the chef hot-smokes tenderloins briefly — 4 to 6 minutes depending on size — with vine cuttings from the vineyard. If you do not have a smoker, purchase the tenderloins at specialty meat markets or use regular tenderloins. Prepare Oven-Dried Damson Plums in advance.

2	pork tenderloins, each 1 to 1 1/2 lb
2	tbsp freshly cracked pepper
1 1/2	tbsp vegetable oil
2	tbsp minced shallots
1	tbsp chopped fresh thyme
2/3	cup Merlot
2/3	cup brown stock
1	cup Oven-Dried Damson Plums (recipe follows)
	salt and pepper

Trim any fat from tenderloins; tuck tail under so meat is of uniform thickness, tying with kitchen string if necessary. If smoking, prepare hot-smoker with grapevine cuttings or other scented wood, such as applewood. For 1 lb tenderloins hotsmoke for 4 minutes, 1 1/2 lb tenderloins 6 minutes. Remove tenderloins and pat dry.

Sprinkle pepper on sheet of waxed paper; lightly roll tenderloins in pepper to coat. Shake off excess. In large heavy-based skillet, heat oil over medium-high heat; sear tenderloins on each side and transfer to ovenproof baking dish. Bake in 425°F oven for 12 to 15 minutes or until internal temperature reaches 160°F or until juices run clear when pork is pierced and just a hint of pink remains inside. Let stand for 10 minutes.

Meanwhile, return skillet used to sear pork to medium-high heat; briefly sauté shallots and thyme. Deglaze skillet with wine, stirring often, for about 8 minutes or until reduced to syrup. Add brown stock and Oven-Dried Damson Plums and reduce to consistency of sauce. Season with salt and pepper to taste.

TO SERVE: Slice tenderloins into 1 1/2-inch thick medallions and spoon plum sauce over top. *Serves 6.*

Wine suggestion — 2000 Sumac Ridge Merlot

---

1 1/2	lb Damson plums (or plums of choice)
2	tsp granulated sugar

Oven-Dried Damson Plums

Slice plums in half and discard pits. Line large baking sheet with parchment paper and place plums, cut side up, on sheet; sprinkle with sugar. Bake in 170°F oven for about 3 hours or until plums have shrunk by half. Let cool. Transfer to plate and set aside. *Makes 1 cup.*

CHANTERELLE-STUFFED VENISON MEDALLIONS WITH THREE-PEPPERCORN SOY VINAIGRETTE

HERALD STREET CAFFE, VICTORIA, BC / *Executive Chef: Mark Finnigan*

Mark Finnigan prefers to use fresh local organic produce and meats in his food preparation at the Herald Street Caffe. This recipe, featuring British Columbia venison, offers a delicious "hint of the wild" in a refined setting. Prepare pâté and peppercorn sauce one day in advance.

2 1/4	lb fresh venison, cut in 6-oz medallions
	Chanterelle Pâté (recipe follows)
1 to 2	tsp vegetable oil
	Three-Peppercorn Soy Vinaigrette (recipe follows)
2	tbsp butter

Make horizontal slit in side of each medallion to form small pocket. Fill each medallion with 2 to 3 oz pâté; let stand for 1 hour.

In skillet, heat oil over medium-high heat; sear medallions, turning once. Transfer to baking sheet and bake in 425°F oven for 6 to 8 minutes or until medium-rare.

Meanwhile, heat prepared peppercorn sauce in same skillet over low heat; add butter and cook until reduced to a shiny glaze. Remove from heat and keep warm.

TO SERVE: Place medallions on warmed plates and drizzle with Three-Peppercorn Soy Vinaigrette. *Serves 6.*

Wine suggestion — 2001 Mission Hill "Estate" Syrah

1	tsp vegetable oil
1	tsp butter
1	leek (white part only), sliced
1	cup fresh chanterelle mushrooms
1	cup white mushrooms
1	cup bread crumbs
3/4	cup chestnut purée*
2	tbsp Madeira
1	tsp dried sage
	pinch each salt and pepper

Chanterelle Pâté

In skillet, heat oil and butter over medium heat; sauté leek and mushrooms until golden. Stir in bread crumbs, chestnut purée, wine, sage and season with salt and pepper to taste.

Transfer mixture to food processor; process until smooth. Refrigerate until ready to use. *Makes 2 1/2 cups.*

*Chestnut purée is available in the specialty section of supermarkets.

1	cup white wine
1/2	cup packed brown sugar
1/2	cup soy sauce
1	tsp minced garlic
1	tsp grated gingerroot
2 to 3	tbsp cracked black, green and pink peppercorns

Three-Peppercorn Soy Vinaigrette

In small saucepan over medium heat, combine wine, sugar, soy sauce, garlic, ginger and peppercorns; simmer, stirring often, for 15 minutes. Remove from heat and let cool. Refrigerate until ready to use. *Makes 1 1/2 cups.*

ROASTED GARLIC CHICKEN AND GRILLED VEGETABLES

IL GIARDINO AND UMBERTO'S, VANCOUVER, BC / *Owner: Umberto Menghi*

This recipe turns an ordinary roast chicken entrée into a delicious medley of Mediterranean flavours and aromas with the addition of grilled vegetables infused with rosemary and thyme.

3 to 4	lb whole chicken
	salt and pepper
10	sprigs fresh thyme
1 1/2	tbsp extra-virgin olive oil
4	large garlic cloves, skins on
	Grilled Vegetables (recipe follows)

Remove all visible fat from chicken; wash inside and out and dry with paper towels. Lightly season chicken cavity with salt and pepper; stuff with thyme. Spread oil evenly over chicken skin. Place chicken and garlic cloves in cast-iron skillet; bake in 375°F oven, basting every 15 minutes with pan juices, for 1 1/4 to 1 1/2 hours or until meat thermometer registers 185°F. Let stand for 10 minutes before carving.

TO SERVE: Place Grilled Vegetables on large warmed platter. Arrange chicken pieces and garlic over vegetables. *Serves 4 to 6.*

Wine suggestion — 2002 Gehringer Brothers "Private Reserve" Pinot Blanc

1/4	cup extra-virgin olive oil
2	sprigs fresh rosemary, chopped
1	tbsp chopped fresh thyme
2	sweet red or green peppers
2	zucchini
1	eggplant
4	tomatoes

Grilled Vegetables

In shallow dish stir together oil, rosemary and thyme. Let stand for 30 minutes or until flavours are blended. Cut peppers in half lengthwise and remove seeds; in pot of boiling water, blanch peppers for 2 minutes. Drain. Cut peppers and zucchini in large strips and eggplant and tomatoes in 1/4-inch slices; brush vegetables with flavoured oil.

Transfer vegetables to greased grill over medium-high heat; cook for 4 to 8 minutes, turning often, or until al dente. Remove individual slices as they reach desired doneness and keep warm.

CHICKEN CURRY

BENGAL LOUNGE AT THE FAIRMONT EMPRESS, VICTORIA, BC / *Executive Chef: David Hammonds*

The Fairmont Empress was named in honour of Queen Victoria, the ruling matriarch of the British Commonwealth when the hotel opened in 1908. In keeping with its British colonial heritage, the Bengal Lounge features an à la carte menu and curry luncheon buffet with an East Indian flavour. Serve with basmati rice and assorted condiments and chutneys, such as the Mount Currie Rhubarb and Sweet Ginger Chutney found on page 113.

3	tbsp vegetable oil
2	tsp minced garlic
2	tsp minced gingerroot
4	lb chicken pieces (legs, thighs, breasts), skin removed
2	tbsp medium curry powder
2	bay leaves
2	tsp ground cumin
1	tsp ground coriander
1	tsp turmeric
1	cup chicken stock
1/2	cup chopped onion
1/2	cup chopped celery
1/2	cup chopped carrot
1/2	cup chopped tomato
1	apple, peeled, cored and diced
2	tbsp tomato paste
2	tbsp lemon juice
	salt and pepper

In large ovenproof saucepan heat oil over medium-high heat; cook garlic and ginger for 1 to 2 minutes. Brown chicken on all sides. Transfer to plate and set aside.

Add curry powder, bay leaves, cumin, coriander and turmeric to saucepan; sauté, stirring, for 1 minute, being careful not to burn. Add stock, onion, celery, carrots, tomato, apple, tomato paste, lemon juice, and salt and pepper to taste; bring to boil. Reduce heat and simmer, stirring often, for 5 minutes. Return chicken pieces to saucepan; cover and bake in 375°F oven for 30 minutes, turning the chicken occasionally. Uncover and cook for 5 minutes longer. *Serves 4.*

Wine suggestion — 2002 Quails' Gate "Limited Release" Gewurztraminer

COQ AU VIN WITH BRAISED GREENS

THE AMPHORA TAPAS BAR AT HAINLE VINEYARDS ESTATE WINERY, PEACHLAND, BC

Chef David Forestell's bold use of unusual herbs and spices in this traditional French recipe will fill your kitchen with inviting aromas on a cool autumn or winter day. Serve the dish over a bed of noodles.

1/2	lb lean bacon, finely chopped
8	shallots or pearl onions, peeled
2	onions, diced
1/4	cup liquid honey
2	tbsp coarsely ground pepper
3 to 4	lb chicken pieces (legs, thighs, breasts) skin removed and trimmed of fat
	salt and pepper
1	can (28 oz) crushed Italian plum tomatoes
2	cups chicken stock
1	bottle (750 ml) Pinot Noir wine
3	bay leaves
4	sprigs savory (or 1/2 tsp dried)
6	juniper berries
1	whole clove
3	star anise*
1/2	cinnamon stick
1/2	orange, cut in 2 wedges
1	lb fall greens (kale, rhubarb chard, mustard or beet in a combination), washed and coarsely chopped

In large heavy-based ovenproof saucepan, cook bacon over medium-high heat until crisp. With slotted spoon, transfer to large bowl and set aside. Drain all but 2 tbsp fat from pan; sauté shallots and onions over medium-high heat for 2 to 3 minutes or until beginning to brown. Add honey and pepper; cook for about 15 minutes or until onions are caramelized. Add onions to bacon in bowl.

Season chicken pieces with salt and pepper. In same pan on high heat, brown chicken in batches, adding additional bacon fat if necessary to prevent sticking. Remove and add to bacon and onion. Add tomatoes and stock to pan and cook over medium-high heat, stirring occasionally, until liquid is reduced to one-quarter of its volume. Add wine to pan along with reserved chicken, onions and bacon; bring to boil. Remove from heat. Add bay leaves, savory, juniper berries, clove, star anise, cinnamon stick and orange wedges; cover and bake in 350°F oven for 1 1/2 hours or until liquid is reduced and thickened sufficiently to add "shine" to chicken. (Dish can be prepared to this point up to 24 hours in advance, covered and refrigerated; reheat in oven.)

About 15 minutes before serving, poke greens into liquid around chicken and return pan to oven. Before serving, remove bay leaves, star anise, cinnamon stick and orange segments. *Serves 4 to 6.*

*Found in Asian Food stores and some supermarkets.

Wine suggestion — 2002 Hainle Vineyards Zweigelt

HERB-CRUSTED RACK OF LAMB

THE TEAHOUSE RESTAURANT IN STANLEY PARK, VANCOUVER, BC / *Executive Chef: Lynda Larouche*

French-style roasted rack of lamb is a classy entrée to serve guests or family for a special occasion. If you are lucky, you will be able to obtain fresh local lamb, but if not, purchase frozen New Zealand lamb from the frozen foods section of your supermarket. Honey Wine Sauce is a delicious accompaniment and is equally good with grilled steak.

1/2	cup bread crumbs
1	tbsp each chopped fresh rosemary, thyme and parsley (or 1 tsp each dried)
1	tbsp minced garlic
1	tbsp butter
2	racks of lamb, each 12 to 14 oz
1	tbsp vegetable oil
1/4	cup Dijon mustard
	salt and pepper
	Honey Wine Sauce (recipe follows)

In bowl, combine bread crumbs, rosemary, thyme, parsley, garlic and butter; set aside. Trim any fat from lamb.

In ovenproof skillet or roasting pan heat oil over medium-high heat; briefly sear lamb racks on both sides. Remove from heat. Brush lamb with mustard; season with salt and pepper to taste. Press crumb mixture into meaty side of lamb. Bake in 375°F oven for 25 to 30 minutes for rare, or until desired doneness. Remove from oven and let stand for 5 minutes.

TO SERVE: Slice lamb between bones. Pour Honey Wine Sauce in centre of warmed plates. Arrange 3 to 4 ribs per serving on pool of sauce. *Serves 4.*

Wine suggestion — 2000 Sumac Ridge "Black Sage" Cabernet Sauvignon

1	cup dry white wine
1/2	cup 35% cream
1	tbsp minced shallot
1	tsp liquid honey
1	tbsp cornstarch
1	tsp water

Honey Wine Sauce

In small saucepan, whisk together wine, cream, shallot and honey; bring to boil. Reduce heat to low. Whisk cornstarch with water and whisk into sauce; cook, whisking, until thickened. Remove from heat and keep warm. *Makes 1 cup.*

SMOKED SALMON–STUFFED CHICKEN BREAST IN PHYLLO WITH SOUR CHERRY GINGER GLAZE

GOOD LIFE BOOKSTORE CAFÉ, SOOKE, BC / *Owner/Executive Chef: Ricardo Monteiro*

This entrée — smoked salmon stuffed in succulent chicken and wrapped in crunchy phyllo — takes a little more time to prepare but the result is well worth the effort. Chef Monteiro uses sour cherries for the glaze when they are available in the spring, but you may substitute other berries and fruits in season.

2	tsp olive oil
3	oz hickory-smoked salmon, chopped
3	oz spinach, blanched and chopped
3	oz fresh wild mushrooms of choice, sliced (or regular button mushrooms, sliced)
1/2	tsp dried basil
1/2	tsp dried thyme
1/2	tsp dried oregano
	salt and pepper
4	boneless skinless chicken breasts, each 6 oz
8	sheets phyllo pastry
1/4	cup butter, melted
	Sour Cherry Ginger Glaze (recipe follows)

In skillet, heat oil over medium heat; sauté salmon, spinach, mushrooms, basil, thyme and oregano, stirring for about 4 minutes or until mushrooms are softened and flavours are blended. Season with salt and pepper to taste. Let cool and set aside.

Butterfly chicken breasts and pound with chef's mallet to uniform thickness. Place one-quarter of the salmon mixture on each breast; fold into package, pressing edges to adhere.

Keeping remaining phyllo covered to prevent drying out, place 1 phyllo sheet on work surface; brush with butter. Place second sheet on top and brush with butter. Place 1 chicken breast on 1 short edge of phyllo; wrap phyllo around breast, folding in sides to form neat package. Brush with butter and place on baking sheet. Repeat with remaining phyllo, butter and breasts. Bake in 375°F oven for about 18 minutes or until firm to the touch and phyllo is golden.

TO SERVE: Arrange phyllo-wrapped breasts on warmed plates (whole or sliced on the diagonal). Drizzle with warm Sour Cherry Glaze. *Serves 4.*

Wine suggestion — 2002 Stag's Hollow "Simply" Merlot

1/2	lb sour cherries, pitted
1	tbsp orange zest
1	cup orange juice
1/2	cup water
1	tbsp granulated sugar
1	tsp grated gingerroot
	lemon juice (optional)*

Sour Cherry Ginger Glaze

In saucepan, bring cherries, orange zest and juice, water, sugar, gingerroot, and lemon juice (if using) to boil; cook, stirring, until reduced to desired consistency. *Makes about 1 cup.*

*If using sweeter fruit for glaze, you may want to add lemon juice to increase tartness.

CRANBERRY-STUFFED PORK TENDERLOIN IN PHYLLO

THE OLD HOUSE RESTAURANT, COURTENAY, BC / *Chef: Trevor Schneider*

Pork tenderloin is one of the easiest cuts of meat to prepare and serve. It is low in fat, exceptionally tender and lends itself to a variety of preparations. This variation, featuring a creamy cranberry filling encrusted in crispy phyllo, makes a fine dinner presentation. Accompany with vegetables of choice.

1	pork tenderloin, 1 1/2 lb
2	tbsp olive oil
3/4 cup	cream cheese, at room temperature
1/2 cup	dried cranberries, coarsely chopped
1/4	tsp salt
1/4	tsp pepper
1/4	tsp cayenne pepper
8	sheets phyllo pastry
1/2 cup	butter, melted

Trim fat from tenderloin. In heavy-based skillet, heat oil over medium-high heat; sear tenderloins on all sides. Transfer to plate and let cool to room temperature.

Meanwhile, in bowl, mix together cream cheese, cranberries, salt, pepper and cayenne pepper until smooth; set aside.

Cut tenderloin in 4 equal portions. Lay 1 sheet of phyllo on work surface, keeping remainder covered to prevent drying out; brush lightly with butter. Lay second sheet on top and brush with butter. Centre 1 piece of tenderloin at short edge of phyllo; spread with 1/4 of the cranberry mixture. Roll up phyllo around tenderloin to make neat package, stopping halfway to tuck in sides. Brush with butter. Repeat with remaining phyllo, butter and tenderloins.

Place packages on ungreased baking sheet; bake in 350°F oven for 15 to 20 minutes or until phyllo is browned and just a hint of pink remains inside pork. (Watch carefully as phyllo burns easily.)

TO SERVE: Carefully cut tenderloin crosswise into 1/2 inch thick slices and arrange on warmed plates. *Serves 4.*

Wine suggestion — 2001 Tinhorn Creek Pinot Noir

VEAL WITH LEMON CAPER SAUCE

BORGO ANTICO RISTORANTE, VANCOUVER, BC / *Owner: Umberto Menghi*

Veal traditionally marries well with lemon and this recipe is no exception: succulent, tender veal simmers in a creamy lemon caper sauce. Medallions of veal tenderloin are used for this recipe at Borgo Antico. For ease in purchasing we have used veal scaloppine with excellent results. Serve with steamed vegetables and roasted new potatoes.

1	lb veal scaloppine
	salt and pepper
1/2	cup all-purpose flour
1	tbsp olive oil
1/4	cup dry white wine
	juice of 1/2 large lemon
1	cup rich homemade chicken stock*
1	tbsp capers, drained

Season veal with salt and pepper; dredge in flour to coat. Heat large skillet over medium heat and drizzle with enough oil to lightly cover surface; sear veal briefly on each side. Transfer to plate and keep warm.

Deglaze pan with wine; stir in lemon juice. Add chicken stock and capers; cook until reduced slightly. Return veal to pan and cook for 3 to 5 minutes or until veal is medium. Transfer to warmed serving dish. Continue cooking sauce, stirring, until reduced to desired thickness.

TO SERVE: Pour sauce over veal. *Serves 4.*

*You can substitute 2 cups canned low-sodium chicken broth cooked until it is reduced by half.

Wine suggestion — 2002 Lake Breeze Semillon

EDGEWATER MARINATED VENISON MEDALLIONS

EDGEWATER LODGE, WHISTLER, BC / *Executive Chef: Thomas Piekarski*

Edgewater's venison is farm-raised on the lodge's own ranch — Ruddock's Gold Pan Ranch near Lillooet, about a two-hour drive north of Whistler. It is as fresh as can be and unbelievably succulent. Chef Thomas Piekarski serves this entrée with a shiitake, green peppercorn and cognac sauce or cranberry sauce. You can use the Spicy Cranberry Sauce on page 16.

1/2	cup vegetable oil
6	cloves garlic, quartered
2	tbsp dry red wine
1	tsp fresh chopped rosemary
1/2	tsp pepper
2	bay leaves
4	pieces fresh venison, each 3 to 5 oz
1	tsp olive oil
1 to 2	tbsp Dijon mustard
2	cloves garlic, minced

In bowl, whisk together vegetable oil, garlic, wine, rosemary, pepper and bay leaves.

Lightly pound venison with meat hammer against the grain until 1 inch thick. Add to bowl and marinate in refrigerator overnight.

Remove venison from marinade shaking off excess. In skillet, heat olive oil over high heat; pan-sear venison on both sides until desired rareness. Remove from heat; brush medallions with Dijon mustard and top with garlic. *Serves 4.*

Wine suggestion — 2000 Sumac Ridge (red) Meritage

HAY-ROASTED FRASER VALLEY POUSSINS WITH CREAMY PARMESAN POLENTA

THE WILDFLOWER RESTAURANT AT FAIRMONT CHATEAU WHISTLER RESORT / *Executive Chef: Glenn Monk*

From the kitchen at Chateau Whistler Resort comes this novel poultry dish featuring individual young chickens roasted on fresh hay. (Ensure that the hay you use is pesticide-free.) The restaurant makes a special effort to use local ingredients and obtains succulent young poultry from producers in the Fraser Valley, southeast of Vancouver. If unable to find young chickens (poussins), substitute Cornish hens. Serve seasonal vegetables alongside.

1	lb fresh dry hay
6	poussins (or 6 small Cornish hens)
	salt and pepper
	assorted sprigs fresh herbs (thyme, basil, rosemary, marjoram, etc.)
1	apple or pear, peeled and cut in small wedges
1	tbsp extra-virgin olive oil (approx)
1	bulb garlic
	Creamy Parmesan Polenta (recipe follows)

Soak hay in water for 5 minutes; drain and spread in bottom of large roasting pan.

Season poussins inside and out with salt and pepper. Fill cavities with a few of the herb sprigs and apple wedges; brush birds with some of the oil. Arrange birds on hay, leaving space between them.

Remove loose skin from garlic bulb; snip top of bulb to expose ends of individual cloves and rub entire surface with olive oil. Separate individual cloves and place around birds along with remaining herbs. Bake in 425°F oven for 25 to 35 minutes or until juices run clear when birds are pierced. Remove from oven and let stand for 10 minutes; remove any hay that is stuck to birds.

TO SERVE: Present poussins "family-style" on large platter with herbs and roasted garlic. (or remove breast meat from bone) and remove legs and thighs; divide among warmed dinner plates along with herbs and garlic.) Accompany with Creamy Parmesan Polenta. *Serves 6.*

Wine suggestion — 2001 Gray Monk "Odyssey" Pinot Gris

4	cups vegetable stock (or water)
1	cup yellow cornmeal
1/3	cup butter
1 1/3	cups grated Parmesan cheese
	salt and white pepper

Creamy Parmesan Polenta

In saucepan, bring vegetable stock to boil. Gradually stir in cornmeal, whisking constantly; reduce heat and simmer for 15 minutes, stirring occasionally.

Gradually add butter and Parmesan, stirring until blended. Season with salt and pepper to taste. Pour into individual buttered ramekins or medium casserole dish. Let stand for 10 to 15 minutes or until polenta is firmly moulded. Invert onto dinner plates or large serving dish. *Serves 6.*

BRAISED RABBIT WITH WILD MUSHROOMS, FRESH HERBS AND MASCARPONE POLENTA

THE MAHLE HOUSE RESTAURANT, NANAIMO, BC / *Owner/Chef: Maureen Loucks*

At the Mahle House Restaurant the chef uses front and back legs from 3 rabbits in this recipe, reserving the loins to grill with a Dijon mustard sauce. For the home kitchen we have adjusted the recipe to use 1 to 2 rabbits. If using rabbit stock prepare it one day in advance to allow flavours to blend.

1 or 2	rabbits (3 to 4 lb total)
2	tbsp unsalted butter
2	tbsp olive oil
1	large onion, diced
3 to 4	cloves garlic, minced
12	oz fresh chanterelle mushrooms, sliced (or mushrooms of choice, sliced)
3	cups Rabbit Stock (recipe follows)*
3	tbsp chopped fresh rosemary, thyme and sage
	salt and pepper
	Mascarpone Polenta (recipe follows)

Remove loins and front and back legs from rabbit(s); reserve remainder for stock.

In skillet, heat butter and oil over medium-low heat: sauté rabbit pieces for 4 to 5 minutes, stirring, until golden brown. Transfer to large baking pan. In same skillet and adding more butter and oil if necessary, sauté onion, garlic and mushrooms, stirring often, for 5 minutes or until softened and browned. Pour in Rabbit Stock and cook until reduced slightly; stir in rosemary, thyme and sage. Season with salt and pepper to taste.

Pour mushroom mixture over rabbit; cover pan with foil and bake in 375°F oven for 1 hour or until well braised. Transfer rabbit to plate and keep warm. Pour braising liquid into saucepan; bring to boil and reduce, stirring, until sauce is thickened.

TO SERVE: Arrange rabbit on warmed plates, top with sauce, and accompany with Mascarpone Polenta alongside. *Serves 4.*

*Chicken stock or mild beef stock may be substituted for rabbit stock.

Wine suggestion — 2001 Quails' Gate "Family Reserve" Pinot Noir

---

2	quarts water
	reserved rabbit
2	onions, chopped
2	carrots, chopped
1	stalk celery, sliced
3	cloves garlic, minced
1/2	tsp salt
1/2	tsp pepper

Rabbit Stock

In large saucepan, combine water, rabbit, onions, carrot, celery, garlic, salt and pepper; bring to boil. Reduce heat to simmer and cook, stirring occasionally, until reduced by half. Strain stock; adjust seasoning if necessary and set aside in refrigerator. Extra stock may be frozen for later use. *Makes 1 quart.*

2 cups water
2 cups whole milk
1 cup yellow cornmeal
2 oz mascarpone cheese
1/4 to 1/2 cup 35% cream
    salt and white pepper

Mascarpone Polenta

In saucepan, bring water and milk to boil. Gradually stir in cornmeal, whisking constantly; reduce heat and simmer for 15 minutes, stirring occasionally. Stir in cheese and enough cream to make smooth texture. Season with salt and pepper to taste.

Pour into individual buttered ramekins or medium casserole dish. Let stand for 10 to 15 minutes or until polenta is firmly moulded. Invert onto dinner plates or large serving dish. *Serves 4 to 6.*

SEAFOOD ENTRÉES

LUCKY ARE THE RESIDENTS OF AN AREA WITH A LONG OCEAN COASTLINE FOR THEY ARE ABLE TO REAP THE FRESH BOUNTY the sea has to offer.

The chefs featured in this book delight in creating innovative seafood dishes with traditional and not-so-traditional ingredients and they generously share some of their finer recipes with us. Whether you prefer your seafood grilled, baked, smoked, sautéed, poached or even raw, you will find a recipe in this collection to tempt your palate. Seafood is often the easiest and quickest of entrées to prepare. For Grilled Fillet of Wild Salmon with Summer Salsa from The Latch Country Inn and Halibut Poêle with Lemon Potatoes and Hollandaise Sauce from La Rua Restaurante, it takes only a few minutes to cook the fish and just slightly longer for the sauces and vegetables.

A number of recipes reveal the Asian influence in Pacific Northwest cuisine: Pan-Charred Rare Tuna with Grotto-Style Sesame Sauce from The Grotto and Good Night Salmon from Tojo's Restaurant are delicious and well worth trying. Many of the recipes, such as Brioche and 7 C's Spice–Crusted Pacific Lingcod and Smoked Black Alaska Cod with Grainy Mustard Dill Beurre Blanc, include seasonings and sauces that are interchangeable and work well with a variety of seafood and meats.

◀ Halibut Poêle with Lemon Potatoes and Chive Butter Sauce

HALIBUT POÊLE WITH LEMON POTATOES AND CHIVE BUTTER SAUCE

LA RUA RESTAURANTE, WHISTLER, BC / *Executive Chef: Tim Muehlbauer*

Halibut marries well with citrus flavours, and Tim Muehlbauer's accompaniment of citrus-flavoured Yukon gold potatoes provides a unique accent. Serve seared Roma tomatoes and steamed asparagus alongside.

1 1/2 to 2 lb halibut fillets each 6 oz
1   cup fish stock
2   tbsp butter
    Lemon Potatoes (recipe follows)
    Chive Butter Sauce (recipe follows)

On grill over high heat, briefly sear fish to mark. Transfer to baking dish; pour in stock and dot fish with butter. Bake in 350ºF oven for 10 minutes or until fish is opaque and flakes easily. Set aside and keep warm. Drain stock into small saucepan over medium heat; cook, stirring often, until reduced by half.

TO SERVE: Arrange Lemon Potatoes in centre of plates. Drizzle Chive Butter Sauce around potatoes and sprinkle with chives. Place fish on top of potatoes and drizzle with reduced stock. *Serves 4 to 6.*

Wine suggestion — 2002 Arrowleaf Cellars Auxerrois

---

2   lb Yukon gold potatoes, peeled and cut in 1/2-inch cubes
    zest and juice of 1 each lime, lemon and orange

Lemon Potatoes

In saucepan, combine potatoes and lime, lemon and orange zest and juice. Pour in enough water to cover potatoes; bring to boil. Reduce heat and simmer for 8 to 10 minutes or until potatoes are cooked but still firm. Remove from heat and let stand in cooking water for 30 minutes. Drain and serve. *Makes 5 to 6 cups.*

1/2   cup unsalted butter
2   tsp lemon juice
2   tbsp chopped chives

Chive Butter Sauce

In small saucepan, heat butter over low heat stirring frequently, until it turns light golden and gives off a nutty fragrance. Carefully stir lemon juice into butter; stir in chives. *Makes 1/2 cup.*

1912 SCALLOP AND PRAWN SAUTÉ

THE HISTORIC 1912 RESTAURANT AND COUNTRY INN, KALEDEN, BC / *Owners: Donna and Allan Dell*

The Dells take full advantage of the fresh produce grown in the Okanagan Valley and change their recipes to accommodate what is in season. If pears are not "ripe from the tree," they recommend substituting the freshest fruit you can find.

2	tsp extra-virgin olive oil
1	lb jumbo prawns, peeled and deveined
1	lb large sea scallops
2	tbsp cold butter
2	tsp minced garlic
2	green onions, julienned
1	cup julienned leek (white part only)
2	Bartlett pears, peeled and sliced
1/2	cup Sumac Ridge Gewürztraminer (or other sweet white wine)
2	tbsp lemon juice
	pinch each dried basil, tarragon, oregano and thyme
	salt and pepper
4 to 5	cups cooked basmati rice or other long-grain rice

In large skillet, heat oil over medium-high heat; sear scallops and prawns. Transfer to plate and keep warm. Add half of the butter, garlic, onions, leek and pears; sauté, stirring, for 3 to 4 minutes or until slightly softened. Return seafood to pan and deglaze with wine and lemon juice. Add basil, tarragon, oregano and thyme and bring to boil; stir remaining butter into sauce to thicken. Season with salt and pepper to taste.

TO SERVE: Spoon seafood over rice. *Serves 4 to 6.*

Wine suggestion — 2002 Sumac Ridge "Private Reserve" Gewürztraminer

SCALLOPS NAPOLEON

THE MAHLE HOUSE RESTAURANT, NANAIMO, BC / *Owner/Chef: Maureen Loucks*

Chef Maureen Loucks loves to create from basics, using fresh local ingredients to full advantage. The restaurant's own organic kitchen garden supplies her with an incredible variety of gourmet vegetables. This seafood entrée has great visual appeal and will delight your palate with its contrasting textures and flavours. Make Lemon Oil one week in advance or use commercially prepared lemon oil.

1 to 2	yams, enough for 12 1/4-inch thick slices (or sweet potato)
1	tbsp unsalted butter
1	tbsp olive oil
1 1/2 lb	large scallops (10 to 20 count)
	Sherried Shiitake and Brown Mushroom Confit (recipe follows)
	Lemon Oil (recipe follows)

Prick yams with fork; microwave at high for 6 to 8 minutes until almost cooked. Let cool. Carefully peel yams and slice each into 12 rounds each about 1/4 inch thick. Transfer to grill over medium heat and cook for 2 to 4 minutes or until tender and slightly browned. (Or in lightly greased skillet over medium heat, sauté slices for 2 to 4 minutes or until browned.) Set aside and keep warm.

In large skillet, heat butter and olive oil over medium-high heat: sauté scallops for 8 to 10 minutes or until opaque, being careful not to overcook.

TO SERVE: Place yam slice in centre of each plate. Top with 1 tbsp Sherried Shiitake and Brown Mushroom Confit. Place 2 or 3 scallops on confit and top with another yam slice. Drizzle Lemon Oil around scallops. *Serves 4 to 6.*

Wine suggestion — 2002 Summerhill "Platinum Series" Pinot Gris

---

Sherried Shiitake and Brown Mushroom Confit

1 1/2	tsp olive oil
1	tsp butter
3	shallots, minced
1/2	lb cremini mushrooms (or cultivated white mushrooms) chopped
1/4	lb shiitake mushrooms, chopped
1/2	cup chicken stock
2	tbsp medium dry sherry
	salt and pepper

In skillet, heat oil and butter over medium-low heat; sweat shallots until softened. Raise heat to medium. Add cremini and shiitake mushrooms; cook, stirring often, for 4 to 6 minutes or until softened. Add stock and simmer, stirring, for 5 to 6 minutes or until thick and rich. Stir in sherry, and salt and pepper to taste. *Makes 2 cups.*

1 cup vegetable oil

2 tbsp olive oil

zest and juice of 3 lemons

pinch turmeric (optional)

Lemon Oil

Use lemon-flavoured oil in salads and to sauté chicken or fish.

In blender, combine vegetable and olive oils, lemon zest and juice and turmeric; process until blended. Funnel into bottle and store in refrigerator for 1 week to infuse flavours. Let come to room temperature. (At this point the oil will separate.) Carefully remove oil from liquid, discarding liquid. Strain oil through fine sieve; return to bottle and refrigerate. *Makes 1 cup.*

AL GRANCHIO (BLACK SQUID PASTA WITH DUNGENESS CRAB SAUCE)

QUATTRO AT WHISTLER, WHISTLER, BC / *Executive Chef/Manager: Rob Parrott*

This entrée makes a very dramatic presentation with its fresh black squid-ink pasta topped with a delicate slightly pink sauce. Try to locate fresh squid-ink fettuccine; if unable, substitute regular semolina fettuccine.

1	tbsp butter
1/4	up finely diced onion
1	tbsp minced garlic
1/2	lb fresh Dungeness crabmeat
1/4	cup brandy
1	cup 35% cream
1/2	cup tomato sauce
1/3	cup chopped fresh basil
	pinch red pepper flakes
	salt
1	lb fresh squid-ink fettuccine

In heavy-based skillet heat butter over medium heat; sauté onion and garlic, stirring often, until softened but not browned. Add crabmeat and sauté until heated through. Pour in brandy and flambé, stirring, until all flames subside. Add cream, tomato sauce, basil and red pepper flakes; simmer for about 5 minutes or until reduced slightly. Season with salt to taste.

Meanwhile, cook fettuccine according to package directions until al dente.

TO SERVE: Divide fettuccine among warmed plates and top with sauce. Garnish with basil. *Serves 4.*

Wine suggestion — 2002 Inniskillin "Dark Horse" Pinot Blanc

SEARED MEDALLION OF SMOKED ALASKAN BLACK COD WITH POTATO ARTICHOKE HASH AND SCALLION OIL

DIVA AT THE MET, VANCOUVER, BC / *Executive Chef: Michael Noble*

Chef Michael Noble has created an updated version of the traditional smoked cod fish and potato dinner: cook the cod to perfection, dress it with a unique potato and artichoke hash, and drizzle with Scallion Oil.

When purchasing, look for "natural smoked cod" which is not over-salted. If the cod is too salty, place in bowl and pour enough milk over fish just to cover. Refrigerate 4 to 8 hours to leach out excess salt; drain and pat dry.

4	smoked Alaska black cod fillets, each 6 oz (optional Atlantic smoked cod)
1	tbsp olive oil
2	tsp butter
	pepper
	Potato Artichoke Hash (recipe follows)
	Scallion Oil (recipe follows)

In skillet, heat oil and butter over medium-high heat; sauté fish until opaque and slightly caramelized. Season with pepper to taste.

TO SERVE: Divide Potato Artichoke Hash among plates, top with fish and drizzle with Scallion Oil. *Serves 4.*

Wine suggestion — 2002 Township 7 Chardonnay

---

1 1/2	lb baking potatoes, peeled and diced
3	tbsp unsalted butter
1/2	cup finely diced red onion
1	sweet red pepper, finely diced
4	fresh artichoke bottoms, trimmed, poached and diced (or 4 canned, diced)
2	cloves garlic, minced
1	tbsp chopped fresh chervil (or 1 tsp dried)
1	tbsp chopped fresh parsley (or 1 tsp dried)
	salt and white pepper

Potato Artichoke Hash

In saucepan, blanch potatoes in boiling water until tender. Drain well. In skillet, heat butter over medium heat; sauté diced potato until slightly browned; add onion and red pepper and additional butter if necessary; cook for 2 to 3 minutes or until golden. Near end of cooking add artichokes, garlic, parsley, chervil and salt and pepper to taste. *Makes 4 to 5 cups.*

4	green onions (green part only), coarsely chopped
1/2	cup extra-virgin olive oil
	pinch ground white pepper

Scallion Oil

In bowl, stir together green onions, oil and pepper; refrigerate for at least 2 hours or for up to 5 hours. Transfer to blender and purée. Taste and adjust seasoning if necessary. *Makes 1/2 cup.*

GRILLED HALIBUT T-BONE WITH SUMMER VEGETABLE SALAD AND CRÈME FRAÎCHE MOUSSE

THE AERIE RESORT, MALAHAT, BC / *Chef de Cuisine: Chris Jones*

Chef de cuisine Chris Jones insists that only the freshest of local produce and seafood be served from the kitchen at The Aerie. In this entrée, he features mild-flavoured Pacific halibut accompanied by a salad of fennel-flavoured local baby vegetables.

2 halibut steaks, each 1 lb
1 tbsp olive oil
1 cup crème fraîche*, whipped
2 tbsp fresh fennel buds (optional)
Summer Vegetable Salad (recipe follows)
olive oil (cold-pressed or extra virgin)
salt and cracked black pepper
4 sprigs each fresh tarragon and fennel frond

Preheat one side of grill to high. Cut halibut steaks in half through centre bone. Brush fish with oil and grill for 2 to 3 minutes per side. Transfer to unheated side of grill; close lid and cook for 2 to 3 minutes longer. Transfer to plate and keep warm.

If using fennel buds, fold into whipped crème fraîche.

TO SERVE: Arrange Summer Vegetable Salad in centre of plates, top with fish and spoon dollop of crème fraîche on fish. Drizzle oil around salad; season with salt and pepper to taste, and garnish with tarragon and fennel fronds. *Serves 4.*

*Traditional crème fraîche is sold in some specialty markets but is also easy to duplicate at home. In a glass bowl, stir together 1 cup 35% cream and 2 tbsp buttermilk. Cover and let stand at room temperature for at least 8 or up to 24 hours. When thick, stir, cover and refrigerate for up to 10 days.

Wine suggestion — 2001 Sumac Ridge "Private Reserve" Sauvignon Blanc

2 cups shaved fennel bulb
1 1/2 cups yellow baby beets, blanched and thinly sliced
1 1/2 cups new potatoes, cooked and thinly sliced
1 tbsp olive oil
salt and pepper

Summer Vegetable Salad

In bowl, combine shaved fennel, baby beets and potatoes; toss with oil until just coated. Season with salt and pepper to taste. *Makes 5 cups.*

COCONUT MILK AND MASALA MUSSELS

BIN 941 TAPAS PARLOUR, VANCOUVER, BC / *Owner/Chef: Gord Martin*

At BIN 941 fresh mussels are prepared in four ways, each highlighting the cuisine of a distinct region. From the menu, chef Martin chose this slightly sweet and aromatic Thai variation for you to re-create at home. Accompany the mussels with warm focaccia or other bread.

3 to 4	lb mussels
3	tbsp extra-virgin olive oil
1	large leek (white part only), julienned
1	cup canned coconut milk
3/4	cup dry white wine
1	tbsp lemon zest (thinly grated)
1/2	tsp garam masala*
	pinch red pepper flakes

Scrub mussels and remove beards. Discard any that have broken shells or that do not close when tapped. In a large saucepan, heat oil over medium heat; sauté leeks briefly. Stir in coconut milk, wine, lemon zest, garam masala and red pepper flakes; bring to a boil. Add mussels, cover and steam for 3 to 5 minutes or until mussels are opened. (Discard any that have not opened.)

TO SERVE: Arrange mussels in individual bowls and pour sauce over top. *Serves 4 as main course or 6 as an appetizer.*

*Garam masala is a traditional Indian seasoning of dry-roasted ground spices from the northern regions of the country. It is available in the gourmet section of some supermarkets or at Indian markets.

Wine suggestion — 2001 Kettle Valley Gewürztraminer

BRANZIO ALLA CROSTA (CRUSTED SEA BASS)

QUATTRO AT WHISTLER, WHISTLER, BC / *Executive Chef/Manager: Rob Parrott*

This recipe is probably the most popular entrée at Quattro at Whistler. Though the restaurant's menu changes quarterly, this dish has remained the top seller during the past three years. Halibut, haddock or any other firm white fish works equally well in this recipe.

1 1/2	lb sea bass piece, skin removed
3	tbsp olive oil
2	cloves garlic, crushed
	salt and pepper
1	cup pistachio nuts, ground
	Roasted Sweet Pepper Sauce (recipe follows)

Cut fish into 4 portions. Whisk together oil, garlic, salt and pepper; brush over fish. Dredge fish in ground pistachios, pressing to adhere. Place in ovenproof skillet and bake in 400°F oven for 10 minutes or until fish is opaque and flakes easily.

TO SERVE: Place fish on warmed plates, drizzle with Roasted Sweet Pepper Sauce and accompany with vegetables of choice. *Serves 4.*

Wine suggestion — 2002 Mission Hill "Reserve" Pinot Gris

Roasted Sweet Pepper Sauce

1	sweet red pepper
1	sweet yellow pepper
1/4	cup chopped fresh basil
1	tsp minced garlic
1/4	cup fish stock
1/4	cup 35% cream
	salt and pepper

On baking sheet, roast red and yellow peppers in 425°F oven for 15 minutes or until skins begin to wrinkle and bracken. Transfer to bowl, cover with plastic wrap and set aside for 30 minutes.

Peel peppers and remove membranes and seeds; in food processor, purée until smooth. Add basil, garlic, fish stock and cream; purée until blended. Season with salt and pepper to taste. Transfer sauce to small saucepan and simmer over medium heat, stirring often, for 10 minutes or until slightly thickened. *Makes 2 cups.*

ALMOND GINGER–CRUSTED CHILEAN SEA BASS WITH ORANGE LIME BEURRE BLANC

RIMROCK CAFÉ, WHISTLER, BC / *Owner/Chef: Rolf Gunther*

The firm yet moist texture of this ocean fish, lightly crusted with a nutty ginger batter and drizzled with orange lime butter sauce, garners rave reviews.

4 to 6	sea bass fillets, each 6 oz
	salt and pepper
1	tbsp lemon juice
1/2	cup almonds, chopped
1	tbsp cornstarch
1	tbsp minced shallots
1	tbsp grated gingerroot
1	egg white
1/4	cup sake (Japanese wine)
1 1/2	tbsp vegetable oil
1 1/2	tbsp butter
	Orange Lime Beurre Blanc (recipe follows)
	thin slices orange and lime

Season sea bass with salt and pepper and drizzle with lemon juice. In bowl, combine almonds, cornstarch, shallots and gingerroot. Whisk egg white with sake until frothy; stir in almond mixture until combined. Dip 1 side of each fillet into batter, coating well.

In heavy-based skillet, heat oil and butter over medium-high heat; fry fish, batter side down for 5 minutes until golden brown. Carefully turn over and cook until fish is opaque and flakes easily.

TO SERVE: Place fish, crust side up, on warmed plates; drizzle with Orange Lime Beurre Blanc and garnish with orange and lime slices. *Serves 4 to 6.*

Wine suggestion — 2002 Mount Boucherie "Estate Collection" Riesling

Orange Lime Beurre Blanc

3/4	cup orange juice
1/3	cup lime juice
3	tbsp 35% cream, whipped
1/2	cup cold butter, cubed

In small saucepan over medium heat, stir together orange and lime juices; cook, stirring occasionally, for about 15 minutes or until reduced to syrupy consistency. Add whipped cream and cook for about 5 minutes or until reduced by half. Whisk in butter, 1 cube at a time, until melted and sauce is creamy. Keep warm until serving. *Makes 1 cup.*

PAN-CHARRED RARE TUNA WITH GROTTO-STYLE SESAME SAUCE

THE GROTTO, NANAIMO, BC / *Owner: Mike Yoshida, Chef: Dave Armour*

The secret to a succulent tuna dish is to purchase the fish as fresh and as thick as possible, then cook it over very high heat to rare or medium rare, ensuring that moisture is retained.

1 1/2	lb tuna piece, (approx 1 inch thick)
1/2	head Boston or Bibb lettuce
1	green onion, chopped
	Grotto-Style Sesame Sauce (recipe follows)

On barbecue or grill over high heat, cook fish, turning once, for 3 to 5 minutes for rare, or 5 to 7 minutes for medium-rare. Slice thinly.

TO SERVE: Arrange lettuce on large plates. Fan tuna slices over top and drizzle with Grotto-Style Sesame Sauce. *Serves 4.*

Wine suggestion — 2001 Mission Hill "Reserve" Merlot

2	tbsp sesame seeds, toasted*
1/4	cup light soy sauce
3	tbsp mirin (Japanese rice wine)
1 1/2	tsp wasabi powder (or 1/2 tsp wasabi paste)
	pinch dashi**

Grotto-Style Sesame sauce

With mortar and pestle, lightly crush sesame seeds. In food processor, combine crushed sesame seeds, soy sauce, mirin, wasabi powder and dashi; process until consistency of sauce. Cover and refrigerate until serving. *Makes 1/2 cup.*

*Toast sesame seeds in dry skillet over medium heat, shaking gently, for 3 to 4 minutes until golden.

**Japanese dried fish–based soup stock

SOOKE HARBOUR HOUSE STEAMED SKATE WING WITH CRANBERRY VINEGAR SAUCE

SOOKE HARBOUR HOUSE, SOOKE, BC / *Luncheon Chef: Pia Carroll*

The chefs at Sooke Harbour House revel in experimentation and love to weave unusual ingredients into their recipes. Skate, also known as ray, are kite-shaped bottom-feeding fish with edible, wing-like pectoral fins. The flesh is sweet with a texture not unlike scallops. If unable to obtain skate wing, you may want to serve the Cranberry Vinegar Sauce with poached halibut or salmon.

1 1/2	lb skate wing, skin and bone removed
	Cranberry Vinegar Sauce (recipe follows)

Divide skate into 4 6-oz portions. In steamer or large saucepan with steaming basket, bring small amount of water to boil over medium-high heat; add skate, cover and cook for 4 to 5 minutes or until opaque throughout. Remove with slotted spatula and let drain on paper towel.

TO SERVE: Pour Cranberry Vinegar Sauce on warmed plates and place skate wings on top. *Serves 4.*

Wine suggestion — 2001 Jackson-Triggs "Proprietors Grand Reserve" Blanc de Noir

---

1	cup fish stock
1/2	cup dry white wine
1	clove garlic, minced
1	shallot, minced
1/3	cup Cranberry Vinegar (recipe follows)
1/3	cup unsalted butter

Cranberry Vinegar Sauce

In heavy-based saucepan, bring fish stock, wine, garlic and shallot to boil over high heat; cook, stirring often, until reduced to syrupy consistency. Add Cranberry Vinegar and cook for 1 minute. Remove from heat and gradually whisk in butter. Set aside and keep warm. *Makes 3/4 cup.*

1	cup fresh or frozen cranberries
1/2	cup white wine vinegar or pure apple cider vinegar

Cranberry Vinegar

This flavoured vinegar is great to have on hand for salad dressings or to accompany fish dishes in lieu of lemon wedges. For a larger yield, simply increase the amount of cranberries and vinegar proportionately. Make it at least one day in advance to allow flavours to blend.

In saucepan, bruise cranberries with wooden spoon, being careful not to mash. Pour in vinegar; bring to boil, stirring, over high heat. Remove from heat and let stand 10 minutes.

Pour vinegar through fine-mesh sieve into bowl. When cool, funnel into sterilized bottles and seal. Store in cool, dark place.

SMOKED BLACK ALASKA COD
WITH GRAINY MUSTARD DILL BEURRE BLANC

SEASONS RESTAURANT IN QUEEN ELIZABETH PARK, VANCOUVER, BC / *Executive Chef: Pierre Delacote*

Black Alaskan cod, also referred to as butterfish and sablefish, lends itself well to smoking. Chef Delacote suggests serving potatoes mashed with garlic and olive oil with this rustic dish.

4 to 6	boneless skinless smoked Alaskan black cod fillets*, each 6 oz (optional Atlantic smoked cod)
	milk
	Grainy Mustard Dill Beurre Blanc (recipe follows)
	thinly sliced red onion rings
2	tbsp capers, drained
	fresh dill sprigs

In shallow pan, pour enough milk over fish just to cover; bring to boil. Reduce heat to medium-low, cover and simmer for 8 to 10 minutes or until opaque. Drain and remove any milk residue from fillets.

TO SERVE: Place fillets on warmed plates; coat with Grainy Mustard Beurre Blanc and top with onion rings, capers and dill sprigs. Accompany with vegetables of choice. *Serves 4 to 6.*

Some varieties of smoked cod are very salty. To reduce saltiness, place cod in bowl, cover with milk and refrigerate for 4 to 8 hours. Drain and proceed with recipe.

Wine suggestion — 2001 Cedar Creek "Platinum Reserve" Chardonnay

1	cup dry white wine
1/2	cup white wine vinegar
1/4	cup minced shallots
3/4	cup chilled unsalted butter, cubed
2	tbsp grainy Dijon mustard
2	tsp hot Dijon mustard
1	tbsp chopped fresh dill (or 1 tsp dried dillweed)
1	tsp liquid honey
	salt and pepper

Grainy Mustard Dill Beurre Blanc

In small saucepan, stir together wine, vinegar and shallots; bring to boil and cook, stirring often, until reduced by one-third. Reduce heat to low to keep sauce hot without simmering. Whisking constantly, add cubes of butter 1 at a time, stirring until melted and sauce is light and creamy. Whisk in grainy and hot Dijon mustards, dill, honey, and salt and pepper to taste. *Makes 1 1/2 cups.*

CEDAR-INFUSED B.C. SALMON WITH ONION CONFIT AND HAZELNUT AND BALSAMIC VINAIGRETTE

VAL D'ISÈRE RESTAURANT, WHISTLER, BC / *Owner/Chef: Roland Pfaff*

Part of the delight of this dish is the aroma that wafts through your kitchen from the baking cedar plank. Roland Pfaff serves his delicately flavoured salmon entrée over a scattering of sautéed sea asparagus accompanied by colourful Sun-Dried Tomato Risotto (see page 108). Sea asparagus grows in the cold waters of the North Pacific and can be purchased in specialty markets throughout the Pacific Northwest.

1	untreated cedar plank*
1 1/2	lb salmon fillets (with skin), 6-oz portions
1	tsp olive oil
	Onion Confit (recipe follows)
	Sautéed Sea Asparagus (recipe follows)
	Hazelnut Vinaigrette (recipe follows)
1/3	cup chopped toasted hazelnuts
	fresh herbs

Soak cedar plank in water for 4 to 6 hours. Lightly brush skin side of salmon with oil. Heat grill to high; briefly sear skin side of fish to mark. Place fish, skin side down, on cedar plank and bake in 375°F oven for 8 to 10 minutes. Top fish with Onion Confit; bake for 1 minute or until fish is medium-rare. Gently slide knife between salmon and skin to separate.

TO SERVE: Centre skin, crunchy side up on plates; scatter sea asparagus over plate. Cut fish portions into 3 or 4 medallions and arrange over skin. Drizzle with Hazelnut Vinaigrette, sprinkle with toasted hazelnuts and garnish with fresh herbs. *Serves 4.*

*Look for an untreated cedar fence board at hardware stores or in lumber yards and ask to have it cut to desired lengths.

Wine suggestion — 2001 Quails' Gate "Family Reserve" Chardonnay

---

2/3	cup water
2	tbsp red wine vinegar
1	sweet onion, chopped
	dash grenadine (or drop red food colouring)

Onion Confit

In saucepan over medium-low heat, stir together water, wine, onion and grenadine; simmer for about 20 minutes or until onions are very tender. Set aside. *Makes 1 cup.*

---

	small bunch sea asparagus
1	tsp olive oil

Sautéed Sea Asparagus

In pot of boiling water, blanch asparagus; drain and pat dry. In skillet, heat oil over medium heat; sauté asparagus, stirring often, until barely tender. Set aside. *Makes 1 cup.*

4   tbsp hazelnut oil

2   tbsp balsamic vinegar

2   tbsp fish stock

Hazelnut Vinaigrette

In blender, mix together oil, vinegar and fish stock. Set aside.
Makes 1/2 cup.

CIN CIN POACHED SALMON WITH SORREL SAUCE

CIN CIN, VANCOUVER, BC / *Executive Chef: Romy Prasad*

Salmon is probably the best-known variety of fish in the Pacific Northwest, and every restaurant has its own special preparation. This delicate poached version from the kitchen of Romy Prasad is easy to prepare and tastes wonderful.

6	cups water
1	cup dry white wine
1/2	stalk celery, sliced
1/2	carrot, sliced
1/4	cup diced onion
1	small lemon, thinly sliced
1	tsp salt
1	tsp coriander seeds
5	sprigs fresh cilantro
5	sprigs fresh parsley
3	sprigs fresh thyme
5	sprigs fresh dill
1/2	cup white wine vinegar
4	salmon fillets, each 6 oz
	Asparagus, Sweet Pepper and Tomato Salad (recipe follows)
	Sorrel Sauce (recipe follows)

In large saucepan, combine water, wine, celery, carrot, onion, lemon slices, salt, coriander seeds, fresh cilantro, parsley, thyme and dill; bring to boil. Reduce heat and simmer for 10 minutes. Add vinegar and simmer for 5 minutes longer. Gently place fish in bouillon; return to simmer, cover and poach for 8 to 10 minutes or until opaque.

TO SERVE: Divide salad among plates; with slotted spoon, transfer fish to top of salad and top with Sorrel Sauce. *Serves 4.*

Wine suggestion — 2002 Jackson-Trigg's (white) Meritage

1	tomato, seeded and diced
1/2	sweet red pepper, diced
1/2	sweet green pepper, diced
4	asparagus spears (tender part only), thinly sliced
1	small bunch watercress

Asparagus, Sweet Pepper and Tomato Salad

In bowl, combine tomato, red and green peppers, asparagus and watercress. Set aside until serving. *Makes 3 to 4 cups.*

Sorrel Sauce

If fresh sorrel is unavailable you may substitute watercress, but the flavour will be more subtle.

1	egg
2	cups fresh sorrel
1/2	tsp vinegar
	generous dash Tabasco Sauce
1/4	cup grapeseed oil
	salt and pepper

In food processor, combine egg, sorrel, vinegar and Tabasco: process until smooth. With machine running, add oil in slow steady stream, processing until slightly thickened. Cover and refrigerate; remove from refrigerator 10 minutes before serving to let come to room temperature. Taste and adjust seasoning with salt and pepper if necessary. *Makes 3/4 cup.*

GRILLED FILLET OF WILD SALMON WITH SUMMER SALSA

THE LATCH COUNTRY INN, SIDNEY, BC / *Innkeeper: Heidi Rust*

The kitchen at The Latch Country Inn specializes in European cuisine highlighted with fresh British Columbia ingredients. The special emphasis on lighter, healthier fare is evident in the perfect balance of this salmon and fresh salsa entrée. Complete the course with roasted baby red-skinned potatoes and a medley of steamed vegetables. If you like a grilled appearance to your salmon, quickly sear fillets on grill for 1 minute before baking.

4	wild salmon fillets, each 5 oz
2	tbsp lemon juice
	salt and pepper
	Summer Salsa

Brush salmon with lemon juice and sprinkle with salt and pepper. Place in ovenproof dish and bake at 400°F for 6 to 8 minutes or until opaque and flakes easily.

TO SERVE: Place fish on warmed plates; spoon Summer Salsa alongside. *Serves 4.*

Wine suggestion — 2002 Tinhorn Creek Pinot Gris

1/4	cup olive oil
1/4	cup minced shallots
1	tbsp lemon zest
2	tbsp lemon juice
12	oz cherry tomatoes, quartered
1/2	English cucumber, peeled and diced
1/4	cup red onion, diced
1/2	large yellow pepper, diced
2	tbsp capers, drained
1	tbsp cilantro, chopped

Summer Salsa

In small bowl, whisk together oil, shallots and lemon zest and juice until well blended. In large bowl, combine tomatoes, cucumber, onion, yellow pepper, capers and cilantro; pour dressing over top and stir to combine. *Makes 4 to 5 cups.*

◀ The Butchart Gardens, Victoria, British Columbia

STILTON-CRUSTED SALMON FILLET WITH WARM CAPER RELISH AND SWEET SOY GLAZE

THE WESLEY STREET, NANAIMO, BC / *Executive Chef: Ian Ter Veer*

Topped with pungent Stilton cheese and a sweetened soy glaze, this is truly salmon with a difference. At The Wesley Street, it is served with creamy horseradish mashed potatoes.

4	sockeye salmon fillets, each 7 oz
	salt and pepper
4	oz Stilton cheese
	Sweet Soy Glaze (recipe follows)
	Warm Caper Relish (recipe follows)

Season salmon with salt and pepper to taste. Crumble Stilton over each fillet, pressing lightly to adhere. Place fish on baking sheet and bake in 400°F oven for 5 to 10 minutes until medium-rare or desired doneness.

TO SERVE: Place fish on warmed plates, drizzle with Sweet Soy Glaze and garnish with Warm Caper Relish. *Serves 4.*

Wine suggestion — 2000 Cedar Creek "Estate Select" Pinot Noir

1	bunch green onions, chopped
1/2	small red onion, chopped
1	small sweet red pepper, diced
1/2	cup sweet white wine
	zest and juice of 1 lime
3	tbsp liquid honey
1/4	cup capers, drained
1/4	cup ketjap manis*

Warm Caper Relish

In skillet over medium low heat, sauté onions and red pepper until tender-crisp. Transfer to bowl and set aside. Deglaze skillet with wine and lime juice and zest: cook, stirring often, until reduced by half. Add wine mixture to onion mixture along with honey, capers and ketjap manis; stir to combine. Keep warm until serving. *Makes 2/3 cup.*

1/4	cup ketjap manis*
1	tbsp wasabi powder
	salt and pepper

Sweet Soy Glaze

In small saucepan, stir together ketjap manis, wasabi powder, and salt and pepper to taste; bring to gentle boil and cook, stirring, until reduced slightly. Remove from heat and keep warm until serving. *Makes 1/4 cup.*

*Ketjap manis, a thick, sweet Indonesian sauce, is available in Asian markets.

WILD SALMON AND SORREL WITH FRESH GINGER JUICE SAUCE

HERALD STREET CAFFE, VICTORIA, BC / *Executive Chef: Mark Finnigan*

This creation from the kitchen of Mark Finnigan makes an impressive presentation. The salmon, sealed within its package of curly savoy cabbage, is cooked to perfection. Prepare Fresh Ginger Juice Sauce in advance.

1 1/3	lb salmon
8	sorrel leaves*
4	small sprigs fresh dill
1	head savoy cabbage
2	tbsp unsalted butter, melted
	salt and pepper
1/2	tsp cracked peppercorns
	Fresh Ginger Juice Sauce (recipe follows)
1	tbsp salmon roe or caviar

Cut salmon into 4 squares, each about 2 1/2" by 2 1/2". Place 2 sorrel leaves and 1 sprig dill on each. Set aside in refrigerator.

Discard outer leaves from cabbage; core and carefully remove 10 leaves. In large pot of boiling salted water, cook leaves for 6 to 8 minutes or until softened. Drain and refresh under cold running water; pat dry. Cut 8 of the best leaves into rectangles; brush with butter and season with salt and pepper to taste. Using 2 leaves, lay 1 over the other to form cross. Place salmon package in centre of cross and fold ends over; wrap tightly in plastic wrap and refrigerate. Repeat with remaining cabbage and salmon packages.

In large saucepan with steaming basket, bring small amount of water to simmer; arrange salmon packages in basket, cover and steam for 7 minutes. Remove saucepan from heat and let continue to cook for 3 to 4 minutes.

TO SERVE: Remove wrap from salmon and sprinkle with cracked peppercorns. With very sharp knife, cut each package across centre without cutting through and place on warmed plates. Drizzle with Fresh Ginger Juice Sauce and garnish with salmon roe. *Serves 4.*

If sorrel is unavailable, substitute spinach leaves.

Wine suggestion — 2002 La Frenz Semillon

1/3	cup grated gingerroot
1 1/2	cups boiling water
	pinch cayenne pepper
2	tsp liquid honey
1	tsp unsalted butter

Fresh Ginger Juice Sauce

Place gingerroot in bowl; stir in boiling water and let cool. Strain liquid into small saucepan. Add cayenne pepper and honey; boil until reduced by half. Remove from heat and stir in butter. *Makes 3/4 cup.*

GOOD NIGHT SALMON

TOJO'S RESTAURANT, VANCOUVER, BC / *Restaurateur: Hidekazu Tojo*

This special salmon creation with the romantic name is easy to prepare. You may substitute other fresh fish of your choice.

3	tbsp miso paste*
2	tbsp mirin (Japanese rice wine)
2	tbsp sake (Japanese wine)
1	tbsp granulated sugar
1	tsp ground ginger
	dash cayenne pepper
1 1/2	lb sockeye or spring salmon piece, cut in 6-oz portions
2	green onions, chopped
4	shiitake mushrooms, chopped

In bowl, whisk together miso paste, mirin, sake, sugar, ginger and cayenne pepper until smooth. Place fish in shallow dish; pour marinade over top, coating well on all sides. Cover with plastic wrap and marinate in refrigerator for 8 hours.

Remove salmon from marinade, and transfer to baking dish; cook in 350°F oven for 12 to 15 minutes or until fish is opaque.

TO SERVE: Place on warmed plates and garnish with chopped green onions and shiitake mushrooms. Accompany with vegetables of choice *Serves 4.*

*Fermented soybean paste is available in Asian markets.

Wine suggestion — 2002 Lake Breeze Pinot Gris

BRIOCHE AND 7 C'S SPICE–CRUSTED PACIFIC LINGCOD

C RESTAURANT, VANCOUVER, BC / *Executive Chef: Robert Clark*

C Restaurant specializes in innovative seafood entrées presented in a dramatic fashion. In this recipe, chef Robert Clark transforms cod into an exotically spiced delicacy served on a bed of julienned red pepper and jícama salad. The 7 C's blend of spices works equally well with pork, chicken and other species of seafood.

1/3	cup brioche crumbs* (or soft bread crumbs, preferably sweet)
2	tsp 7 C's Spice Blend (recipe follows)
1/4	tsp salt
1/4	tsp pepper
2	jícama, peeled and julienned
2	sweet red peppers, seeded and julienned
3	tbsp mayonnaise
1	tsp Dijon mustard
1	tbsp butter
1 1/2	lb lingcod fillets (6-oz portions)
2	lemons, halved
	Tomatillo Emulsion (recipe follows)
1	green onion, sliced
2	tbsp diced pickled beets

In bowl, mix together brioche crumbs, 7 C's Spice Blend, salt and pepper; set aside. In separate bowl, combine jícama, red peppers, mayonnaise and mustard; set aside in refrigerator.

In ovenproof skillet, heat butter over medium-high heat; sear cod on 1 side until golden. Turn over and sprinkle with crumb mixture; cook for 3 minutes. Transfer skillet to 375°F oven and bake for 8 to 10 minutes or until crumb mixture is browned and fish is opaque and flakes easily. Remove from oven; squeeze juice of 1/2 lemon over each fillet.

TO SERVE: Arrange salad in centre of plates; top with fish. Drizzle Tomatillo Emulsion around salad and garnish with green onion and diced pickled beets. *Serves 4.*

*Brioche is a sweet French bread made with large amounts of butter and eggs; it is sold in French and specialty bakeries.

Wine suggestion — Domaine de Chaberton Bacchus (dry)

Tomatillo Emulsion

1/2	cup tomatillos*, hull removed, cleaned and diced
2	tbsp vegetable oil
1	tbsp cilantro leaves
	salt and pepper

In blender, purée tomatillos, oil and cilantro until smooth. Season with salt and pepper to taste. Set aside until serving. *Makes 1/2 cup.*

A small fruit popular in Mexican and Southwest cooking, tomatillos, or Mexican green tomatoes, as they are also called, are sold in Latin American and specialty grocery stores and some supermarkets.

---

7 C's Spice Blend

1	tbsp caraway seeds
1	cardamom seeds or ground cardamom
8	whole cloves
2	tbsp ground cumin
2	tbsp ground coriander
1	tbsp chili pepper flakes or powder (ancho, chipotle, red, etc.)
2	tsp cinnamon

In dry skillet over medium heat, toast caraway and cardamom seeds, stirring often to prevent burning, for about 5 minutes or until fragrant. Let cool.

In blender, process seeds, cloves, cumin, coriander, pepper flakes and cinnamon until a fine powder. Let cool and store in airtight container for up to 6 months. *Makes 1/3 cup.*

LUNCH, TEA, BREAKFAST

HERE ARE DELIGHTFUL RECIPES THAT WILL TAKE YOU ON A CULINARY ODYSSEY THROUGHOUT THE DAY, FROM EARLY morning through to afternoon tea.

Chateau Whistler Granola from the slope-side Wildflower Restaurant on Whistler Mountain is filled with nuts, fruits and grains to keep you at a high energy level for hours. For a more leisurely and elegant breakfast/brunch experience, try Orange Cardamom French Toast from Oritalia or Summerhill Smoked Salmon Eggs Benedict from Summerhill Estate Winery.

I have included a trio of creamy rice risottos, each featuring different vegetables: sun-dried tomatoes; chanterelle mushrooms and sweet corn; and pumpkin with saffron. Serve the risottos with a salad and warm crusty bread for a light luncheon.

When you are in the provincial capital, Victoria, you must treat yourself to the experience of afternoon tea at Fairmont Empress. This tradition has been carried on at the hotel for generations, and you are invited to recapture the ritual in your own home with an assortment of teatime recipes.

◀ Empress Scones

ORANGE CARDAMOM FRENCH TOAST

ORITALIA, VANCOUVER, BC / *Executive Chef: Julian Bond*

This variation of your mother's French toast will sweep you off your feet. Its citrus flavour with just a hint of exotic cardamom is simply the best!

8	eggs
3/4	cup 10% cream
3	tbsp orange zest
3/4	cup orange juice
2	tbsp Grand Marnier
1 1/2	tsp ground cardamom
1	loaf white country bread or fruit bread, thickly sliced
2 to 3	tbsp butter
	fresh seasonal berries
	icing sugar
	maple syrup, warmed

In bowl, beat together eggs, cream, liqueur, orange zest, orange juice and Grand Marnier. Stir in cardamom and let stand for 1 hour.

Soak bread slices in egg mixture. In skillet, heat 1 tbsp butter over medium heat; fry bread slices for 2 to 3 minutes per side or until golden and centre is cooked. Repeat for remaining slices adding more butter to skillet as necessary.

TO SERVE: Top French Toast with berries, dusting of icing sugar and warmed maple syrup. *Serves 4 to 6.*

CHATEAU WHISTLER GRANOLA

THE WILDFLOWER RESTAURANT AT FAIRMONT CHATEAU WHISTLER RESORT / *Executive Chef: Glenn Monk*

If all cereal tasted as good as this, then you would rarely find bacon and eggs on the breakfast menu. Wholesome and nutritious, it's just what you need to prepare for a day on the slopes.

4	cups rolled oats
1 2/3	cups chopped pecans
1 1/2	cups wheat bran
1 1/2	cups slivered almonds
1 1/3	cup sunflower seeds
2/3	cup sesame seeds
1/3	cup + 1 tbsp vegetable oil
2 1/2	cups raisins
1 1/2	cups chopped dates
3/4	cup currants
1/3	cup liquid honey
1	tbsp vanilla extract
1	tbsp orange zest

In large bowl, combine rolled oats, pecans, wheat bran, almonds, sunflower seeds and sesame seeds; pour in 1/3 cup oil and stir to coat. Spread on 2 baking sheets; bake in 325ºF oven, stirring every 10 minutes, for 30 minutes or until golden. Transfer to large bowl. Add raisins, dates and currants.

Combine honey, vanilla and orange zest; stir into granola until well combined. Let cool completely before storing in airtight container for up to 1 month. *Makes about 3 1/2 lb or 30 servings.*

FRITTATA TRATTORIA

TRATTORIA DI UMBERTO RESTAURANT, WHISTLER, BC / *Owner: Umberto Menghi*

This traditional Italian omelette sports a goat cheese, mushroom and roasted sweet pepper flavour with just a hint of basil. Serve it for breakfast or add a small salad for a luncheon dish.

1	sweet red pepper
6	eggs
1	tbsp chopped fresh basil (or 1/2 tsp dried)
	pinch salt
	pepper
1	tsp olive oil
1/2	cup button or cremini mushrooms, sliced
1/2	cup goat cheese (chèvre), crumbled

On grill over high heat, roast red pepper, turning often, for 8 to 10 minutes or until skin is charred. Remove from heat and let cool in paper bag. Remove skin; core, and seed. Chop pepper and set aside.

In large bowl, beat together eggs, basil, salt and pepper; set aside. In ovenproof skillet, heat oil over medium heat; sauté mushroom and red pepper for 4 minutes. Stir into egg mixture along with goat cheese.

In same skillet, cook egg mixture over medium heat for 3 minutes. Transfer skillet to 375°F oven and cook for 8 to 10 minutes or until desired firmness is reached. *Serves 4.*

Wine suggestion: Sumac Ridge Private Reserve Pinot Blanc 1999

SUMMERHILL SMOKED SALMON EGGS BENEDICT

SUNSET VERANDA RESTAURANT AT SUMMERHILL ESTATE WINERY, KELOWNA, BC / *Chef: Graham Pierce*

Eggs Benedict is traditionally served with ham and Hollandaise Sauce. But you will never settle for the traditional once you savour Smoked Salmon Eggs Benedict from the kitchen at Summerhill Estate Winery. It is warm and succulent, with a delicious Hollandaise and generous chunks of hot-smoked salmon prepared on site. Serve with a side salad and garnish of choice.

2	English muffins, sliced
	butter
4	oz smoked salmon
	water
1	tsp vinegar
4	eggs
	Hollandaise Sauce (recipe follows)

Lightly toast muffins; spread with butter. Top with smoked salmon and keep warm in oven.

In saucepan large enough to poach all eggs, combine water and vinegar; bring to simmer. Crack eggs and gently slip into water; poach to desired doneness. Remove with slotted spoon, draining excess water. Place on muffins and top with Hollandaise Sauce. *Serves 4.*

Hollandaise Sauce

2	egg yolks
2	tsp white wine
	pinch salt
	dash Tabasco Sauce
1/2	cup clarified unsalted butter, melted

In top of double boiler over simmering water, beat together egg yolks, wine, salt and Tabasco; cook, whisking constantly, for 6 to 8 minutes or until mixture begins to thicken enough to coat back of spoon. Slowly whisk in melted butter. Remove from heat and keep warm. *Makes 3/4 cup.*

Wine suggestion: Summerhill Chardonnay 2000

SPRING MUSHROOM CANNELLONI

THE AERIE RESORT, MALAHAT, BC / *Chef de Cuisine: Chris Jones*

This lunch or light dinner entrée tastes wonderful and, as an added bonus, it makes an interesting presentation for guests. The cannelloni are cut on the bias and positioned to stand up in a splash of herbed stock and rich yellow extra-virgin olive oil.

3	sheets fresh herb pasta, 10 x 4 inches*
3	tbsp vegetable oil
	salt
1	onion, chopped
2	cloves garlic, minced
3	cups chopped mushrooms (combination morel, oyster and/or cremini)
1/2	cup dry white wine
1/2	cup rich chicken stock**
1 1/2	cups coarse bread crumbs
1 1/2	tbsp chopped fresh rosemary
2 or 3	eggs, beaten
	pepper
	Herbed Chicken Stock (recipe follows)
	extra-virgin olive oil
1	cup shaved sheep's milk cheese or Parmigiano-Reggiano cheese

Cut pasta sheets crosswise in 3 equal parts. Fill large pot three-quarters full of water; add 1/2 tsp of the vegetable oil and pinch of salt. Bring to boil. Blanch pasta in boiling water until slightly underdone, 4 to 8 minutes depending on type of pasta. Drain and let cool in ice water. Lightly oil pasta; place on baking sheet, cover with plastic wrap and set aside.

In skillet, heat remaining vegetable oil over medium heat; cook onion and garlic, stirring often, for about 4 to 5 minutes or until softened. Add mushrooms and sauté, stirring constantly, for about 5 minutes or until tender and light golden. Deglaze skillet with wine and chicken stock; continue to cook for about 10 to 12 minutes or until liquid is completely evaporated. Transfer to bowl and let cool. Stir in bread crumbs, rosemary and enough egg to moisten. Season with salt and pepper to taste.

Spoon mushroom mixture along 1 short end of each pasta sheet; roll up to diameter of 1 inch. Wrap each cannelloni tightly in plastic wrap and tie ends with twine to seal cannelloni for final cooking. You will have 9 individual rolls.

Bring large pot of water to boil; add wrapped cannelloni. Reduce heat to simmer and poach for 7 to 10 minutes or until firm. Drain; carefully unwrap cannelloni and keep warm.

TO SERVE: Cut each cannelloni in half on diagonal. Place 6 cannelloni halves, flat end down, upright in centre of each of 6 warmed plates. Lay remaining cannelloni on plates for a total of 3 per serving. Surround with Herbed Chicken Stock and extra-virgin olive oil; top with shaved cheese. *Serves 6.*

*Fresh pasta sheets are available in most food stores.

** To make rich chicken stock, heat canned sodium-reduced chicken broth over medium heat and reduce by half.

---

1 1/2	cups sodium-reduced chicken broth
	handful fresh herbs (any combination of rosemary, oregano, basil, thyme)

Herbed Chicken Stock

In small saucepan, bring chicken broth and herbs to boil; reduce heat to medium-low and simmer until reduced by half. Set aside. Makes 3/4 cup.

SUN-DRIED TOMATO RISOTTO

VAL D'ISÈRE RESTAURANT, WHISTLER, BC / *Owner/Chef: Roland Pfaff*

At Val d'Isère, chef Roland Pfaff serves this risotto as an accompaniment to his cedar-infused salmon entrée. It works equally well as a light vegetarian main course served with a crisp salad and crusty French bread.

4	tbsp unsalted butter
4	tbsp minced shallots
2	tbsp minced garlic
1	cup Arborio rice*
2 1/2 to 3 cups vegetable stock	
3	tbsp tomato paste
3	tbsp chopped dry-packed sun-dried tomatoes
3	tbsp diced tomatoes
3	tbsp grated Parmesan cheese (approx)
	salt and pepper
	sprigs fresh herbs

In saucepan, melt butter over low heat; cook shallots and garlic, covered, for 5 minutes. Add rice and cook, stirring constantly, until grains are slightly transparent. Pour in 1/2 cup vegetable stock; cook, stirring often and adding remaining stock 1/2 cup at a time, allowing rice to completely absorb liquid each time, for about 25 minutes or until rice is almost tender. Add tomato paste and cook for 4 to 5 minutes or until creamy and al dente. Stir in sun-dried tomatoes, diced tomatoes and Parmesan cheese; season with salt and pepper to taste.

TO SERVE: Mound slightly on plates or in shallow bowls; garnish with fresh herbs and additional Parmesan cheese. *Serves 4.*

Italian-grown Arborio rice is thicker and shorter than other short-grain rice and has a higher starch content.

PORTOBELLO MUSHROOM CUTLETS WITH BALSAMIC SAUCE AND ROASTED BABY VEGETABLES

BIN 941 TAPAS PARLOUR, VANCOUVER, BC / *Owner/Chef: Gord Martin*

Chef Gord Martin is skilled at blending diverse flavours, colours and textures in his dishes, turning the ordinary into a memorable repast. This portobello mushroom tapatiser is one of the signature selections at BIN 941.

4	large portobello mushrooms, stems removed
4	tbsp olive oil
2	tbsp balsamic vinegar
	salt and pepper
1	egg
1	cup milk
1/2	cup all-purpose flour
3	cups panko* (or dry bread crumbs)
	Balsamic Sauce (recipe follows)
1	tbsp butter
1	head roasted garlic**
	Roasted Baby Vegetables (recipe follows)

Spread mushrooms on baking sheet: sprinkle with half of the oil, the balsamic vinegar and salt and pepper to taste. Bake in 400°F oven for 10 minutes; turn and bake for 10 minutes longer. Remove from oven and let cool.

Lightly beat egg and milk to make egg wash. Dredge mushrooms in flour, dip in egg wash and coat with panko, pressing to adhere. In large ovenproof skillet, heat remaining oil and add mushrooms; transfer to 425°F oven and bake for 10 minutes. Turn mushrooms and bake for 10 minutes longer or until coating is crisp. Transfer to plate and keep warm.

Heat same skillet over medium heat; cook Balsamic Sauce, butter and roasted garlic, whisking until butter is dissolved.

TO SERVE: Centre mushrooms on each of 4 warmed plates; top with Roasted Baby Vegetables and drizzle with Balsamic Sauce mixture. *Serves 4.*

Panko crumbs are coarse Japanese bread crumbs and are available in Asian markets.

**To roast garlic: Separate and peel cloves of 1 head garlic. Bake on baking sheet in 350°F oven for 20 to 25 minutes until soft and brown.*

1 1/4	cups balsamic vinegar
1	tbsp granulated sugar
1	tsp cornstarch
1 1/2	tbsp water

Balsamic Sauce

In small saucepan over medium heat, cook balsamic vinegar until reduced by half. Combine sugar, cornstarch and water; whisk into vinegar and cook, stirring constantly, for 3 to 5 minutes or until slightly thickened. Set aside. *Makes 2/3 cup.*

Roasted Baby Vegetables

2	tbsp olive oil
2	cups baby vegetables (combination of baby carrots, zucchini and squash), sliced lengthwise
1	cup French beans, sliced lengthwise
2	baby bok choy, sliced
1/2	sweet red pepper, julienned
1	tbsp zatar*

In ovenproof skillet, heat olive oil over medium-high heat; cook baby vegetables, beans, bok choy, red pepper and zatar, stirring to coat, for 2 to 3 minutes. Transfer to 425°F oven and bake, turning occasionally, for 15 minutes or until browned. Set aside and keep warm.

Zatar is a Greek and Middle Eastern seasoning of thyme, salt and sesame seeds found in Mediterranean specialty shops.

CHANTERELLE AND SWEET CORN RISOTTO

BISHOP'S RESTAURANT, VANCOUVER, BC / *Executive Chef: Dennis Green*

This creamy risotto works well as an accompaniment to a favourite entrée or as a main-course vegetarian dish. The beautiful trumpet-shaped chanterelle mushroom is found in the wild in the Pacific Northwest. If fresh chanterelles are not available, you may substitute any of the more exotic wild mushrooms, such as enoki, morel or shiitake, but you will not achieve the delicate light orange colour.

3	tbsp butter
1	cup diced onions
1	large clove garlic, minced
1/4	cup chopped fresh sage
2	cups chanterelle mushrooms
2	cups Arborio rice*
1/2	cup dry white wine
1	cup corn kernels
4	cups chicken stock
1	cup 35% cream
1	cup small fresh spinach leaves
1/4	cup grated Parmesan cheese (approx)
	salt and pepper
	sprigs fresh sage

In saucepan, melt butter over low heat; cook onions, garlic and sage, covered for 5 minutes. Add mushrooms and sauté for 1 to 2 minutes or until lightly coloured. Add rice and sauté for 2 to 3 minutes or until grains are slightly transparent. Deglaze pan with wine. Add corn and enough stock to cover rice by 1/2 inch. Simmer, stirring often and adding more stock as necessary to keep rice covered, for about 30 minutes or until rice is almost tender. Add cream, spinach and Parmesan cheese and cook for 4 to 5 minutes or until creamy but al dente. Season with salt and pepper to taste.

TO SERVE: Mound slightly on serving plates and garnish with sage sprigs and additional Parmesan cheese. *Serves 6.*

Italian-grown Arborio rice is thicker and shorter than other short-grain rice and has a higher starch content.

MOUNT CURRIE RHUBARB AND SWEET GINGER CHUTNEY

THE WILDFLOWER RESTAURANT AT FAIRMONT CHATEAU WHISTLER RESORT / *Executive Chef: Glenn Monk*

It is the policy at Chateau Whistler Resort to utilize locally grown produce whenever possible. This delicious gingery condiment features ripe red rhubarb grown in nearby Pemberton, at the base of snow-capped Mount Currie. It works well as an accompaniment to cheese and crackers, savoury biscuits and with pork, chicken or fish dishes.

4	tbsp vegetable oil
2	cups chopped onion
1 1/2	tsp diced gingerroot
2	tsp minced garlic
2	tsp curry paste*
4	lb rhubarb, peeled and cut into 1-inch cubes
1	cup raisins
1 1/2	cups packed brown sugar
1 1/2	cups cider vinegar
1	tsp salt

In large pot, heat oil over medium heat; sweat onions for 4 to 5 minutes. Add ginger, garlic and curry paste; cook, stirring often, for 4 to 5 minutes or until onions are softened. Stir in rhubarb and raisins; add sugar and stir until dissolved.

Add vinegar and salt; reduce heat to low and simmer for 30 minutes. Remove from heat; pour into hot sterilized jars and seal. *Makes about 6 cups.*

Curry paste is available in the specialty section of most supermarkets and in Asian food stores.

EMPRESS SCONES

AFTERNOON TEA AT THE FAIRMONT EMPRESS HOTEL, VICTORIA, BC / *Executive Chef: David Hammonds*

It's teatime on the West Coast, featuring The Fairmont Empress Hotel's world-famous scones. An institution at The Empress since 1908, this afternoon repast is prepared for more than 100,000 guests annually. The scones are served hot from the oven with thick cream and homemade strawberry preserves.

3	cups all-purpose flour
1/2	cup granulated sugar
2	tbsp baking powder
1/3	cup butter, softened
3	eggs
1	cup 35% cream
1/3	cup raisins
1	tbsp water
	pinch salt

In bowl, sift together flour, sugar and baking powder. Add butter and blend with fingertips until incorporated and mixture is mealy. (Be careful not to overprocess.) Lightly beat 2 of the eggs and blend into mixture along with cream just until combined.

On floured surface, lightly press batter to 1-inch thickness. With biscuit cutter, cut out scones and place on ungreased baking sheet. Whisk together remaining egg, water and salt to form egg wash; brush over scones and let stand for 45 minutes, uncovered.

Bake in 325°F oven for 20 to 25 minutes or until scones are golden brown. *Makes 1 1/2 dozen.*

ALMOND CRACKERS

QUATTRO AT WHISTLER, WHISTLER, BC / *Executive Chef: Rob Parrott*

Chef Rob Parrott serves these delightful little bites with anise pistachio ice cream as an accompaniment to his Chocolate Terrine dessert. They are tasty, appealing to the eye and a versatile addition to a wide variety of desserts as well as to an afternoon tea tray.

2	cups all-purpose flour
1/2	tsp baking soda
	pinch salt
1/3	cup granulated sugar
1/3	cup liquid honey
1/4	cup butter, softened
2	tsp vegetable oil
1	egg white
1 1/2	tsp vanilla extract
1	tsp almond extract
1/4	cup sliced almonds

In bowl, sift together flour, baking soda and salt. Set aside.

Using mixer on medium speed, cream sugar, honey, butter and oil until well blended. Add egg white, vanilla and almond extract; beat just until blended. Stir in flour mixture until combined (dough will be sticky).

Divide dough into 2 equal portions. Shape each into 9-inch log; wrap in plastic wrap and freeze until firm.

Cut each log into 1/4-inch slices and place 1 inch apart on greased baking sheet. Top each with sliced almond, pressing lightly to adhere. Bake in 350°F oven for 6 to 8 minutes or until lightly browned. Transfer to racks and let cool. *Makes 6 dozen.*

DESSERTS

I BELIEVE THAT IT IS IMPOSSIBLE TO CREATE A TRULY DECADENT DESSERT WITHOUT CREAM, BUTTER AND SUGAR. THOSE WHO claim it can be done never seem to be able to completely satisfy the sweet-tooth cravings of true die-hard dessert lovers. My motto is "Indulge with moderation." Serve smaller dessert portions and limit their frequency. Enjoy fresh fruit most days of the week and live it up occasionally with one of these delicious dessert recipes.

Chocolate lovers will rave over the silky smooth Chocolate Terrine from Quattro at Whistler and will testify that Boca Negra from The Mahle House Restaurant has to be the best chocolate cake ever created.

When rhubarb first appears in your garden and at local markets, you know spring is here and summer is not far off. To herald the season, make the sweet little Rhubarb Upside-Down Cakes from Bishop's Restaurant or the Stilton Cheesecake with Rhubarb Compote from Diva at the Met Restaurant. Contributing chefs take full advantage of the wonderful summer fruits and berries available to them in British Columbia and have offered us a variety of delectable ways to enjoy them. Treat family and friends to Fresh Berries with Ginger-Scented Mascarpone, or Stone Fruit Clafouti with Toasted Hazelnuts, which features a trio of fresh Okanagan Valley fruits, from The Amphora Restaurant at Hainle Vineyards Estate Winery.

Many of these recipes include additional sauces, creams and garnishes and I encourage you to be as resourceful as our contributing chefs: mix and match different components and ingredients according to what is in season or what you have on hand. I am sure you will enjoy creating these delicious recipes and that you will make them over and over again.

◀ Sunburnt Lemon Pie

SUNBURNT LEMON PIE

SEASONS RESTAURANT IN QUEEN ELIZABETH PARK, VANCOUVER, BC / *Executive Chef: Pierre Delacote*

Serve this classic dessert garnished with a variety of fresh fruit slices and berries. The fruit will provide a lovely contrast in colour and taste.

1 1/2 cups	all-purpose flour
1/3 cup + 1 tbsp	granulated sugar
1/2 cup	butter, softened
1	egg
1 tsp	orange zest
1 tbsp	orange juice
	Lemon Filling (recipe follows)

Pastry

In bowl, combine flour and 1/3 cup sugar. Mix in butter with fingertips until crumbly, being careful not to overprocess. In small bowl, whisk together egg, orange zest and juice. With fork, stir egg mixture into flour mixture just until ball forms. Wrap in plastic wrap and refrigerate for 20 minutes.

On lightly floured surface, roll out pastry to uniform thickness of 1/4 inch. Press into lightly greased 10-inch pie plate. Cover with parchment paper and fill with pie weights. Bake in 350°F oven for 20 minutes or until centre is set. Lift out parchment with weights. Cool.

Pour Lemon Filling into pastry shell; bake for 30 minutes. Remove from oven and let cool. Cover edges of crust with foil, sprinkle remaining 1 tbsp sugar evenly over tart surface and broil for 3 to 4 minutes or until sugar is caramelized. (Watch carefully to make sure pie does not burn.) *Serves 8 to 12.*

Lemon filling
(prepare while shell is cooling)

6	eggs
3/4 cup	granulated sugar
3/4 cup	35% cream
1 tsp	lemon zest
1/2 cup	lemon juice
1 1/2 tsp	vanilla extract

With mixer, beat eggs and sugar until pale. Add cream, lemon zest and juice and vanilla; beat until smooth. Set aside until pie shell is cooled.

STONE FRUIT CLAFOUTI WITH TOASTED HAZELNUTS

THE AMPHORA TAPAS BAR AT HAINLE VINEYARDS ESTATE WINERY, PEACHLAND, BC

Clafouti, traditionally made with cherries, is varied at The Amphora Tapas Bar to showcase locally grown Okanagan Gold Bar apricots, Red Haven peaches and the highly prized but rare Southern Belle White nectarines.

4	apricots, 2 peaches and 2 nectarines
4	eggs
6	tbsp granulated sugar
3/4	cup milk
2	tbsp Frangelico
2	tsp vanilla
1/2	cup all-purpose flour
	pinch salt
2	tbsp unsalted butter
1/3	cup toasted hazelnuts*, coarsely chopped
1	cup 35% cream, whipped
	icing sugar

Plunge fruit into pot of boiling water for 30 seconds so that skins can be easily removed. Cut apricots into quarters, peaches into eighths and nectarines into sixths. Set aside.

In large bowl, whisk eggs and 4 tbsp of the sugar until volume is almost tripled. Add milk, Frangelico, and vanilla; whisk to combine. Sift flour and salt over top; whisk vigorously until no lumps remain.

Place butter in well-seasoned 10-inch cast-iron skillet; heat in 450°F oven until butter just begins to brown. Remove skillet from oven; quickly pour in batter. Cover with fruit pieces and sprinkle with hazelnuts and remaining sugar.

Return skillet to oven, reduce heat to 400°F and bake for 25 to 30 minutes or until deep golden brown and toothpick inserted in centre comes out clean. Let cool until just warm and serve with dollop of whipped cream and dusting of icing sugar. *Serves 6 to 8.*

*To toast hazelnuts: Spread nuts in single layer on baking sheet; bake in 350oF oven for 10 to 15 minutes or until golden. Immediately wrap in clean tea towel and rub to remove skins. Let cool; chop coarsely.

FRESH BERRIES WITH GINGER-SCENTED MASCARPONE, CITRUS CURD AND PISTACHIO TUILE TOWERS

THE AERIE RESORT, MALAHAT, BC / *Executive Chef: Chris Jones*

This exceptional dessert offers the home chef a variety of options. Each sub-recipe is interchangeable and may be combined with other dessert recipes. For example, the ginger-scented mascarpone can be served alone, accompanied by the citrus curd or a berry coulis. The pistachio towers can be filled with whipped cream, ice cream or a flavoured mousse. The chef notes that some of the recipes will make more than 4 to 6 portions, but this is necessary to successfully complete the recipes. Extra tuiles can be frozen for later use.

	Pistachio Tuiles (recipe follows)
	Ginger-Scented Mascarpone Mousse (recipe follows)
2	cups fresh seasonal berries of choice (raspberries, blueberries, strawberries, blackberries)
	Citrus Curd (recipe follows)
	icing sugar
	mint leaves

Fill tuiles half full with Ginger-Scented Mascarpone Mousse; top with some of the berries. Mound small amount of remaining mousse onto centre of each of 6 dessert plates and stand tuile(s) upright in centre. Garnish with Citrus Curd and additional berries. Dust with icing sugar and garnish with mint. *Serves 6.*

Ginger-Scented Mascarpone Mousse

2	tbsp liquid honey
1	tsp finely minced gingerroot
8	oz mascarpone cheese, at room temperature
1/2	cup 35% cream

In small saucepan, heat honey and ginger over medium heat; cook, stirring, until reduced slightly. Remove from heat and let cool.

Fold honey mixture into mascarpone cheese until well blended. In mixer, whip cream until stiff peaks form; gently fold in mascarpone cheese mixture. Cover and refrigerate until using. *Makes 1 1/2 cups.*

Citrus Curd

	zest and juice of 2 lemons
	zest and juice of 2 oranges
	zest and juice of 1 lime
3/4	cup granulated sugar
6	egg yolks

In top of double boiler over simmering water, whisk together lemon, orange and lime zest and juice, sugar and egg yolks; cook, whisking vigorously, for 8 to 10 minutes or until thickened. Strain through fine-mesh strainer and refrigerate to chill. *Makes 1 1/2 cups.*

Pistachio Tuiles

3/4	cup unsalted butter, softened
1/2	cup granulated sugar
3	egg whites
3/4	cup all-purpose flour
1/4	cup ground pistachio nuts

With mixer, cream butter and sugar until light and fluffy. With mixer running, add egg whites, 1 at a time; gradually add flour until blended. Let stand for 2 to 3 hours.

Line baking sheet with parchment paper. Spread batter on paper in thin 4 x 2-inch rectangles. Sprinkle with pistachio nuts and bake in 350°F oven for 5 to 6 minutes until light golden. Remove from oven; with spatula, quickly lift tuiles from pan and drape each around 3/4-inch diameter dowel, pressing edges to adhere, to create 2-inch high cylinders. Let cool and set aside. *Makes 2 dozen.*

WARM RAIN FOREST CRUNCH BANANA WITH HOT CHOCOLATE SAUCE

HERALD STREET CAFFE, VICTORIA, BC / *Executive Chef: Mark Finnigan*

The combination of crunchy phyllo bananas drizzled in a warm chocolate sauce and nestled against cold ice cream sends taste buds into ecstasy.

1/2 cup toasted pecans*, chopped

1/2 cup toasted coconut*

2 large ripe bananas, peeled and cut in half crosswise

4 sheets phyllo pastry

1/2 cup butter, melted

vanilla bean ice cream

Hot Chocolate Sauce (recipe follows)

icing sugar

In bowl, combine nuts and coconut. Roll banana halves in nut mixture, pressing firmly to coat well. Set aside.

Place 1 sheet of phyllo on work surface and brush with butter. Top with second sheet, brush with butter and cut phyllo stack in half crosswise. Lay 2 of the bananas on ends of phyllo rectangles; roll up, folding in sides. Repeat with remaining phyllo, butter and bananas.

Brush banana rolls with melted butter and bake in 350°F oven for 10 minutes or until pastry is golden brown.

TO SERVE: Cut rolls in half on angle. On each of 4 dessert plates place 1 half upright and another on its side. Scoop vanilla bean ice cream next to rolls. Drizzle with Hot Chocolate Sauce and dust with icing sugar. *Serves 4.*

To toast pecans and coconut: Spread nuts and coconut on separate baking sheets and bake in 350°F oven, stirring or shaking pans often, for 10 to 12 minutes or until golden and fragrant. Let cool.

Hot Chocolate Sauce

5 oz bittersweet chocolate, finely chopped

1 cup 35% cream

2 tbsp unsalted butter

Place chocolate in bowl. Bring cream to boil and pour over chocolate. Add butter and whisk until chocolate is melted. *Makes 1 cup.*

RHUBARB UPSIDE-DOWN CAKES

BISHOP'S RESTAURANT, VANCOUVER, BC / *Executive Chef: Dennis Green*

Rhubarb has traditionally heralded the beginning of spring and the arrival of fresh produce after a lingering winter season. Though treated as a fruit, this tart vegetable is actually a member of the buckwheat family. In this dessert from Bishop's Restaurant, the rhubarb becomes slightly caramelized with the brown sugar when baked in a buttery orange cake. Serve warm with a dollop of whipped cream or vanilla bean ice cream.

1	lb rhubarb
1/4	cup butter, melted
2/3	cup packed brown sugar
1/2	cup butter, softened
1/2	cup granulated sugar
2	eggs
1 1/2	cups all-purpose flour
1	tsp baking powder
1/2	tsp baking soda
1/2	tsp salt
	zest and juice of 1 orange
1/2	cup milk

Cut rhubarb stalks in half horizontally and slice into 1/2-inch pieces. Brush each of 6 large (10 oz) ramekins with melted butter; sprinkle with brown sugar. Cover bottom of ramekins with sliced rhubarb.

In bowl, cream butter and granulated sugar until light and fluffy. Beat in eggs, mixing well. Sift together flour, baking powder, baking soda and salt; mix into butter mixture alternately with orange zest, juice and milk. Fill ramekins two-thirds full with batter; bake in 350°F oven for 25 to 30 minutes or until tops are golden. Let cool for 10 minutes.

TO SERVE: Run sharp knife around edge of each cake to loosen and invert onto individual dessert plates. *Serves 6.*

STILTON CHEESECAKE WITH RHUBARB COMPOTE

DIVA AT THE MET, VANCOUVER, BC / *Executive Chef: Michael Noble*

This is quite possibly one of the best cheesecakes ever! Executive chef Michael Noble marries in perfect harmony his distinctive creamy blue cheese filling with a melt-in-your-mouth buttery crust. This dessert received GQ Magazine's Top Taste Award for 1997 from food writer Alan Richman. Feel free to substitute other seasonal fruit for the rhubarb.

Shortbread Base

1 1/3	cups all-purpose flour
3	tbsp granulated sugar
1/2	cup less 1 tbsp butter, softened

With mixer, blend together flour and sugar. Beat in butter until blended, being careful not to overprocess. Lightly press dough over bottom of greased 8-inch springform pan. Bake in 350°F oven for 8 to 10 minutes or until golden brown. Remove from oven and let cool.

Filling

24	oz cream cheese, softened
4	oz Stilton cheese, softened
1	cup + 1 tbsp granulated sugar
2	tsp vanilla extract
1/3	cup all-purpose flour
4	eggs
1	cup sour cream
	Rhubarb Compote (recipe follows)

With mixer, blend cream cheese, Stilton cheese, 1 cup sugar and vanilla until smooth. Mix in flour, then eggs, 1 at a time, beating well after each addition. Add sour cream and mix until smooth. Pour into cooled crust and bake in 300°F oven for about 1 hour or until centre is just firm to the touch. Remove from oven, run knife around edge of pan and let cool at room temperature. Cover and refrigerate until serving.

To serve, sprinkle cheesecake with remaining 1 tbsp sugar and broil for about 3 to 4 minutes or until lightly browned. (Watch carefully to ensure that top does not burn.) Let sugar topping cool; slice into wedges. Serve with spoonful of Rhubarb Compote. Serves 12 to 14.

Rhubarb Compote

1/2	cup granulated sugar (approx)
1/4	cup port
12	dry pink peppercorns, crushed
3	cups diced rhubarb

In saucepan, combine sugar, port and peppercorns; bring to boil and cook until reduced by half. Add rhubarb, reduce heat to low and simmer until rhubarb is softened slightly. Taste and adjust sweetness if necessary by adding more sugar. Refrigerate until serving. *Makes 2 cups.*

CHOCOLATE TERRINE

QUATTRO AT WHISTLER, WHISTLER, BC / *Executive Chef: Rob Parrott*

This smooth-as-silk dessert is a chocolate lover's dream. The chefs at Quattro at Whistler serve it with almond cookies and pistachio anise ice cream but you can garnish it with crème anglaise, sweetened whipped cream or a fruit sauce.

6	oz semisweet chocolate, chopped
3/4	cup butter, cubed
1 1/2	tbsp very strong espresso coffee
6	egg yolks
3/4	cup superfine sugar*
1	cup cocoa powder, sifted
1 1/2	tbsp Cointreau
2	cups 35% cream

In top of double boiler over simmering water, stir together chocolate, butter and espresso until melted and smooth. Remove from heat.

With mixer, whisk egg yolks and sugar until mixture falls in ribbons. Fold in chocolate mixture until well blended. Fold in cocoa and Cointreau.

Whip cream until stiff peaks form. Gently fold into chocolate mixture. Pour into 8- x 4-inch loaf pan lined with plastic wrap. Cover with plastic wrap and refrigerate for 12 hours.

TO SERVE: Unmould terrine on flat surface; gently remove plastic wrap. Slice into serving-size portions. *Serves 8 to 10.*

*Make your own superfine sugar by processing regular granulated white sugar in a food processor for a few minutes or until crystals are smaller.

NANAIMO BARS

KIPLING'S AT THE FAIRMONT EMPRESS, VICTORIA, BC / *Pastry Chef: Ken Harper*

One could not compile a recipe book of Pacific Coast flavours without including Nanaimo bars, those sweet little chocolate and cream squares that take their name from a city on the east coast of Vancouver Island. Their reputation is so far-reaching that they can be found at bake sales, afternoon teas and wedding receptions from British Columbia to Newfoundland. Nanaimo bars are a Canadian tradition, and this recipe from Kipling's at The Fairmont Empress shows how to prepare them perfectly.

2	cups graham cracker crumbs
1	cup sweetened coconut
1/2	cup chopped walnuts
3/4	cup + 1 tbsp butter
1/4	cup granulated sugar
5	tbsp cocoa powder
1	egg, beaten
1	tsp vanilla extract
2	cups icing sugar
3	tbsp milk
2	tbsp vanilla custard powder*
4	oz semisweet chocolate, chopped

In bowl, combine graham cracker crumbs, coconut and walnuts; set aside.

In top of double boiler over simmering water, combine 1/2 cup of the butter, sugar, cocoa, egg and vanilla; cook, stirring constantly, until mixture is thickened. Stir into crumb mixture; press into buttered 9-inch square cake pan.

With mixer, cream 1/4 cup of the remaining butter, icing sugar, milk and vanilla custard powder until light and creamy; spread over crumb base and refrigerate until hardened.

In top of double boiler over simmering water, melt chocolate and remaining butter, whisking until smooth; drizzle over top of squares. Refrigerate until firm. Cut into squares. *Makes 2 dozen.*

*Vanilla custard power, a combination of cornstarch, salt and vanilla flavouring, is found in the baking section of supermarkets. Most Canadians know the product by the name Bird's Custard Powder.

CARAMELIZED APPLE AND PHYLLO TOWER WITH CRÈME ANGLAISE AND EASY CARAMEL SAUCE

THE WESLEY STREET, NANAIMO, BC / *Executive Chef: Ian Ter Veer*

This impressive dessert is a combination of taste sensations: the crunchiness of phyllo, the sweet-tart flavour of warm apples, the silkiness of crème anglaise and caramel sauce, and cold vanilla ice cream.

2/3 cup butter, melted
2/3 cup granulated sugar
4 sheets phyllo pastry
4 Granny Smith apples
Easy Caramel Sauce (recipe follows)
Crème Anglaise (recipe follows)
vanilla ice cream

Set aside 2 tbsp of the butter and 2 tbsp of the sugar. Place 1 sheet of phyllo on work surface with 1 short edge facing you; butter bottom half of phyllo and sprinkle with sugar. Fold unbuttered half over buttered half and repeat buttering and sugaring one more time until phyllo is folded into quarters. Butter and sugar top of phyllo quarter; cut into 4 equal pieces. Repeat with remaining 3 sheets of phyllo to make a total of 16 layered squares. Place on baking sheets and bake in 375°F oven for 3 to 6 minutes or until golden. (Watch carefully; phyllo burns easily.) Remove from oven and set aside.

Slice top and bottom from apples and slice each into 4 rings of equal thickness. Remove core from centres, being careful not to break rings. In skillet over medium heat, combine reserved butter and sugar. Add apples and sauté until caramelized, turning often for even cooking.

TO SERVE: Place 1 layered phyllo square on each of 4 large dessert plates; top with apple ring. Repeat until there are 4 phyllo-apple layers on each plate. Garnish with Easy Caramel Sauce, Crème Anglaise and vanilla ice cream. *Serves 4.*

2 cups 35% cream
6 egg yolks
2/3 cup granulated sugar
2 tsp vanilla extract

Crème Anglaise

You may create a lighter sauce with less fat content if you substitute milk, 10% cream or a combination for the 35% cream in this recipe.

In top of double boiler over simmering water, heat cream until scalding. In bowl, beat egg yolks and sugar until pale; very gradually add cream, whisking constantly. Return to double boiler; add vanilla and cook, stirring constantly, for about 10 minutes or until thick enough to coat back of spoon. Immediately transfer to bowl and set in pan of ice water to cool, stirring occasionally. *Makes 2 cups.*

Easy Caramel Sauce

1/4 cup butter
1 cup 35% cream
1/2 cup packed brown sugar
2 tbsp light corn syrup
1 tsp vanilla extract

In small saucepan, melt butter over medium heat; add cream, sugar, corn syrup and vanilla and bring to boil, stirring. Boil hard, stirring constantly, for 5 minutes. Let cool for 10 minutes; pour into bowl; cover and refrigerate for up to 1 week. *Makes 1 cup.*

BOCA NEGRA

THE MAHLE HOUSE RESTAURANT, NANAIMO, BC / *Owner/Chef: Maureen Loucks*

Chef Maureen Loucks provided this dessert recipe because she feels that it is incredible and "must be shared." No doubt you will agree it is the best chocolate cake you have ever tasted. A little goes a long way as it is very rich. Prepare the White Chocolate Cream one day in advance to allow flavours to blend.

1 1/3	cups granulated sugar
1/3	cup water
4	tbsp bourbon
12	oz good-quality semisweet chocolate, finely chopped
1	cup unsalted butter, cubed
5	eggs
2	tbsp all-purpose flour
	white and dark chocolate curls for garnish (optional)
	White Chocolate Cream (recipe follows)

In small saucepan over medium heat, stir together sugar, water and bourbon; bring to boil, stirring to dissolve sugar. Remove from heat and keep warm.

In top of double boiler over simmering water, melt chocolate; transfer to food processor. With machine running, gradually pour sugar syrup through feed tube; process until smooth. With machine running, add butter pieces, then eggs, 1 at a time. Add flour and process for 12 seconds.

Lightly grease a deep 9-inch round cake pan; line bottom with parchment or waxed paper and grease paper. Pour batter into prepared pan, running spatula over top to smooth.

Place cake pan in shallow roasting pan. Pour enough boiling water into roasting pan to come 1 inch up side of cake pan. Place roasting pan in centre of 350°F oven; bake for 50 to 60 minutes or until top forms thin, dry crust like a brownie. Remove cake pan from water bath, wipe dry and let cool.

Invert onto flat plate, peel off parchment, and quickly but gently invert onto serving plate (cake may settle at this point) Mound centre of cake with white chocolate curls and sprinkle with chocolate curls.

TO SERVE: Place thin slices of cake on dessert plates with a dollop of White Chocolate Cream. *Serves 10 to 12.*

12	oz white chocolate, finely chopped
1	cup 35% cream
2	tbsp bourbon
2	tbsp Kirsch

White Chocolate Cream

In top of double boiler over simmering water, melt chocolate. In small saucepan, heat cream until scalding; whisk into chocolate, stirring until smooth. Stir in bourbon and Kirsch. Transfer cream mixture to container with tight-fitting lid and refrigerate overnight. Let come to room temperature before using. *Makes 2 cups.*

FRANGELICO MOUSSE WITH CHAMPAGNE SABAYON

THE COUNTRY SQUIRE, NARAMATA, BC / *Owner/Chef: Patt Dyck*

The flavour of this melt-in-your-mouth dessert is best described as "heavenly." The mousse is prepared one day in advance, whereas the romantic Champagne Sabayon is prepared just before serving to ensure its light texture.

1 1/3	cups hazelnuts
4	egg yolks
2/3	cup granulated sugar
1	tsp vanilla extract
1/3	cup Frangelico
1 1/2	cups 35% cream
	Champagne Sabayon (recipe follows)

On baking sheet, toast hazelnuts in 350°F oven for 10 to 15 minutes or until golden. Remove from oven; immediately wrap nuts in tea towel and let steam for 15 minutes. Rub vigorously to remove skins; let cool. Set aside 1/3 cup of the nuts for garnish. In food processor, grind remaining nuts until fine. Set aside.

With mixer, beat together egg yolks, sugar and vanilla until thickened and lemon-coloured. Fold in nuts and Frangelico.

With mixer and clean bowl, beat cream until stiff peaks form; stir half into nut mixture. Fold in remaining cream. Pour mousse into lightly greased 8-oz ramekins, filling two-thirds full. Freeze for about 12 hours or overnight.

TO SERVE: Briefly set each ramekin in hot water to soften slightly. Run knife around mousse and use knife to "pop" out onto dessert plates. Serve with Champagne Sabayon on the side. Garnish with reserved toasted hazelnuts. *Serves 6.*

3	egg yolks
1/4	cup granulated sugar
1/2	cup Champagne

Champagne Sabayon

In top of double boiler over simmering water, beat egg yolks and sugar until foamy and pale. Add Champagne, a little at a time, whisking constantly, until mixture begins to thicken. (Be careful not to overheat as mixture will separate.) Continue whisking until thickened and falls in ribbons. Serve immediately. *Makes 3/4 cup.*

WARM PECAN PIE WITH VANILLA BEAN ICE CREAM

THE LATCH COUNTRY INN, SIDNEY, BC / *Innkeeper: Heidi Rust*

All desserts should be a little bit sinful, and this pecan-filled pie with its warm buttery flavour fulfills that mandate. If you make the pie ahead, warm it slightly before serving with vanilla bean ice cream.

1 1/2	cups all-purpose flour
1	tbsp granulated sugar
1	tbsp vanilla custard powder*
1/3	cup room temperature butter
	ice water

Pastry

In bowl, combine flour, sugar and custard powder; add butter and mix with fingertips until mixture resembles fine crumbs. Gradually add ice water (about 4-5 tbsp) with fingertips until you can form a soft ball. Wrap in plastic wrap and refrigerate for at least 30 minutes.

On lightly floured surface, roll out dough to 1/8-inch thickness. Fit into 9-inch pie plate.

Vanilla custard powder, a combination of cornstarch, salt and vanilla flavouring, is found in the baking section of supermarkets. Most Canadians know the product by the name Bird's Custard Powder.

1	cup brown or granulated sugar**
1	cup corn syrup
1/4	cup butter, melted
3	eggs, lightly beaten
	pinch salt
1 1/2	cups pecans
	pastry shell

Filling

In bowl, stir together sugar, corn syrup, butter, eggs and salt until well combined; mix in pecans. Pour into pastry shell. Bake in 325°F oven for 50 minutes or until golden brown. Remove from oven and let cool until warm. *Serves 8.*

**Pecan pie is traditionally made with brown sugar but you may use white (granulated) if you desire a lighter-coloured pie.*

DELIGHT OF THE KING

THE TEAHOUSE RESTAURANT IN STANLEY PARK, VANCOUVER, BC / *Executive Chef: Lynda Larouche*

These spectacular swan-shaped sweets are almost too pretty to eat! Executive chef Lynda Larouche comments that they have been a favourite at The Teahouse for many years and have been a tradition with newly engaged couples. Do not be daunted by the recipe; the swans are not difficult to make.

1　cup water
1/2　cup butter
3/4　tsp + 1/2 tsp salt
1　cup all-purpose flour
4　eggs + 1 egg
1　cup 35% cream, whipped
　　icing sugar
1 1/2　cups fresh berries of choice
　　Chocolate Sauce (see Warm Rain Forest Crunch Banana with Hot Chocolate Sauce, page 122)

In saucepan over medium-high heat, bring water, butter and 1/2 tsp salt to boil. Remove from heat as soon as liquid boils; add flour all at once and beat vigorously with wooden spoon until mixture is smooth and pulls away from pan. Beat for 30 to 45 seconds over low heat to dry mixture. Remove from heat and let cool slightly.

Beat 1 egg and set aside. Beat 3 of the remaining eggs into warm dough, 1 at a time, beating well after each addition. Beat in just enough of the reserved egg to make very shiny mixture.

Reserve 1 cup of the dough and spoon remaining into pastry bag fitted with star #10 tip. Make swan bodies by piping 10 to 12 ovals, each about 3 x 1 1/2 inches, onto lightly greased baking sheet. Place reserved dough in pastry bag fitted with plain #3 tip. Pipe 15 S-shaped necks, each 3 to 4 inches long, on second lightly greased baking sheet (make extra necks to allow for breakage).

In small bowl, beat remaining 1 egg and remaining 1/2 tsp salt to make egg glaze; lightly brush over bodies and necks. To ensure even rising, gently press each body with back of fork dipped in cold water.

Bake in 400°F oven for 15 minutes or until necks are browned. Remove necks and transfer to racks and let cool. Bake bodies for 10 to 15 minutes longer or until browned. Transfer to racks and let cool.

TO SERVE: Cut swan bodies in half horizontally, then cut each top piece in half lengthwise to form wings. Stir berries into whipped cream; spoon cream mixture into body cavity. Insert neck in cream at 1 end of body. Place wings in cream at an angle so that they spread up and out from neck. Place swans on dessert plates; dust with icing sugar and drizzle Chocolate Sauce around swans. *Makes 10 to 12 swans.*

PROFILES

BC ROCKIES & KOOTENAYS

Naturalists and outdoor sports enthusiasts regard the Rockies and the Kootenays, located in the southeastern area of the province, as their version of "heaven-on-earth." In this country of unsurpassed beauty you can find towering mountains cradling soft valleys, rushing rivers pouring into deep vibrant lakes and cold glacial streams amidst bubbling hot springs. One only has to look at the large number of designated national and provincial parks to realize the ecological significance of the area.

ALL SEASONS CAFÉ

Jonathan Langille and Tracey Scanlan have two loves: good food and the atmosphere of rural British Columbia. How fortunate for diners in the Nelson area that they combined their loves into the All Seasons Café, a fashionable bistro located in the prettiest back alley in the province.

Their innovative fare combines the best of Pacific Northwest cuisine with international touches. The creative seasonal menus use the finest organic produce, meats and seafood and may feature original dishes such as Pacific Crab Cakes with Creamed Cilantro Pesto and Roma Tomato Concasse or Nori-Wrapped BC Halibut with Coconut Curry Sauce on Basmati Rice. Marry this menu with the restaurant's fine selection of VQA British Columbia wines – Wow!

620 Herridge Lane
Nelson, BC, V6L 6A7
Telephone: (250) 352-0101
Web site: www.allseasonscafe.com
Open year-round • Dinner daily
Restaurateurs: Jonathan Langille and Tracey Scanlan

EAGLE'S EYE RESTAURANT
(AT KICKING HORSE MOUNTAIN RESORT)

When you are dining at an elevation of almost 8,000 feet, the view is spectacular, the air is lighter, and the blue sky seems clearer. Constructed in chalet style with natural timber, stone, and sweeping glass windows, the Eagle's Eye definitely gives diners a bird's eye view of the world.

The dining room offers both a luncheon and a fine-dining dinner menu. Evening selections may include Warmed Pepper-Crusted Goat Cheese with herb crostini and black currant conserve and gourmet entrées such as Organic Wild Northern Caribou with sun-dried blueberry jus and baby red nugget potatoes. Follow your repast with a Chocolate and Ginger Truffle Tart or Lemon Berry Napoleon made with fresh seasonal berries.

1500 Kicking Horse Trail
Golden, BC V0A 1H0
Telephone: 1-866-SKI-KICK ext. 5413

E-mail: jlush@kickinghorseresort.com
Web site: www.kickinghorseresort.com
Open-seasonally • Summer: End-June through September • Winter: Mid-December through mid-April • Lunch and dinner daily
Dining room Manager: John Lush • Executive Chef: David Knoop

FAIRMONT HOT SPRINGS RESORT
Including
MOUNTAIN FLOWERS DINING ROOM
TUSCANO'S MARKET

Situated at the base of the mountains with the Columbia Valley and Purcell Mountains to the west, this non-smoking resort is designated a "Power Smart Green Hotel" for its commitment to energy efficiency and environmental responsibility. Operated by the Wilder family since the 1950s, it is dedicated to family recreation. In addition to the hot thermal pools, there is golf, horseback riding, hiking, mountain-biking, skiing and a spa facility. Accommodation is offered in a 140-room lodge. The complex also features an RV Park with 311 sites.

Meals are served in the casual Mountain Flowers Dining Room. A combination of Pacific Northwest and Rocky Mountain cuisine offers patrons the finest fresh local ingredients. Seasonal service is also featured in Tuscano's Market, an informal Italian-style eatery with an open kitchen and oyster bar.

Box 10, Fairmont Hot Springs
BC, V0B 1L0
Telephone: (250) 345-6311 or 1-800-663-4979
E-mail: info@fairmonthotsprings.com
Web site: www.fairmonthotsprings.com
Open: year round • Breakfast, lunch and dinner daily
President: Carol W. Seable • Food & Beverage Manager: Mohsen el Wakeel

FIDDLER'S GREEN RESTAURANT

You will find Fiddler's Green Restaurant a short drive north of Nelson just off Route 3A, the scenic route that borders the western shore of Kootenay Lake. This heritage home with a garden setting features tastefully decorated dining rooms with enchanting window views.

The restaurant is noted for its quality dining, excellent food presentation and attentive service. Find yourself tempted with dishes such as Dungeness Crab Cakes with

saffron vegetable slaw, Stuffed Grilled Eggplant Rolls served with tomato coulis on baked polenta or Lemon and Garlic Grilled Rack of Lamb accompanied by risotto and a selection of fresh vegetables. Desserts made in the restaurant's kitchen include Fiddler's Sinfully Rich Cheesecake and Decadent Chocolate Soufflé. Fiddler's Green offers best British Columbia wines.

2710 Lower Six Mile Road
Nelson, BC V1L 6L4
Telephone: (250) 825-4466
E-mail: mail@fiddlersgreen.ca
Web site: www.fiddlersgreen.ca
Open year-round • Dinner daily (winter season: Wednesday through Sunday only)
Owners: Lynda and Harald Manson

STRAND'S OLD HOUSE RESTAURANT

Strand's Old House Restaurant is in Invermere, a picturesque town nestled among towering snow-capped mountains and overlooking a beautiful valley with a clear, glistening lake.

Built in 1912 as a private home, it was converted to a restaurant in 1980. The historical ambience is preserved in the restaurant's décor and furnishings. Owner and executive chef Tony Wood offers a seasonal set menu complemented by an extensive daily "fresh sheet" highlighting the chefs' creativity with available ingredients. This restaurant, with its casual atmosphere and reputation for well-prepared dishes, is a favourite of locals and visitors. Reservations are advised in summer.

818 12th Street
Invermere, BC V0A 1K0
Telephone: (250) 342-6344
Web site: www.invermere.com/strands/
Open year-round: Dinner daily
Owner/Executive Chef: Tony Wood • Chef: Gregor Zundel

OKANAGAN VALLEY

The Okanagan Valley encompasses a large north-south valley positioned between vast mountain ranges. In a province of extreme mountainous terrain, this valley is an unlikely geographical jewel, with its fertile soil, large recreational lakes and mild, dry climate. Hot summer temperatures and long days of light due to its northern latitude make the Okanagan Valley one of Canada's premier fruit-farming and wine-producing areas.

THE AMPHORA TAPAS BAR

Hainle Vineyards Estate Winery is one of the province's smallest estate wineries, producing approximately 5,500 cases annually.

Food and wine naturally go together — and what better way to pair the wonderful wines of the Okanagan Valley than with foods featuring local ingredients? The Amphora Tapas Bar opened its doors in 1995 after being granted the province's first food licence for wineries.

The restaurant has built a strong reputation, offering diners the best of local products presented in a flavourful and creative manner. The Tapas Bar also offers a catering service and custom dinners.

5355 Trepanier Bench Road
Peachland, BC V0H 1X0
Telephone: (250) 767-2525 or 1-800-767-3109
E-mail: info@hainle.com
Web site: www.hainle.com
Open April through October • Lunch and dinner Wednesday through Sunday

CEDAR CREEK ESTATE WINERY

Family run Cedar Creek Estate Winery, winner of *Access* magazine's "2002 Winery of the Year Award" is set on a vineyard overlooking Lake Okanagan. Food and wine complement each other and the best way to savour Cedar Creek's award winning wines is with a selection of tapas-style dishes served in the Vineyard Terrace Restaurant. Sample fare such as Grilled Vegetable Terrine, Roasted Red Pepper Tapenade and Peppered Rare Beef Salad while you relax on the patio surrounded by the spectacular garden and vineyard.

Tastings are offered every day. The Wineshop sells Cedar Creek wines and a selection of gifts and accessories.

Tours and dining on the Vineyard Terrace are available May through October.

5445 Lakeshore Road
Kelowna, BC V1W 4S5
Telephone: (250) 764-8866
E-mail: info@cedarcreek.bc.ca
Web site: www.cedarcreek.bc.ca
Restaurant open: May to mid-October, 11:30 am – 5:30 pm
President: Gordon Fitzpatrick

CELLAR DOOR BISTRO AND CATERING

Cellar Door Bistro, located on the grounds of the Sumac Ridge Estate Winery, offers guests "the perfect marriage of food and wine." The bistro shares space with the wine shop and tasting centre in a building situated atop a knoll within the winery complex. There is a bustle of activity as each business operates separately, yet symbiotically. Chef Neil Schroeter takes full advantage of this relationship in his selection of dishes that complement and enhance the wines and produce of the region. The restaurant's menu changes monthly to accommodate the finest regional meats, seafood, fruits and vegetables.

The bistro exudes a fresh, functional atmosphere with the creative use of working materials from the winery. The large chandelier and individual corkscrew-style light fixtures are artistically fashioned with the winery's cobalt blue Cuvee Millennium bottles while spent wine corks act as mulch for the flower beds.

Located at Sumac Ridge Estate Winery
17403 Highway 97
Summerland, BC V0H 1Z0

Telephone: (250) 494-0451
E-mail: info@cellardoorbistro.com
Web site: www.sumacridge.com
Open March through December • Lunch and Dinner daily
Restaurateur: Harry McWatters • Executive Chef: Neil Schroeter

FRESCO RESTAURANT

Before opening Fresco Restaurant in the resort city of Kelowna chef Rodney Butters and wife Audrey Surrao embarked on a year of world travel to refine and contemplate their culinary direction. The result of their travels is Fresco, a restaurant that ensures diners experience a meal of excellence in an air of easy relaxation.

The atmosphere at Fresco Restaurant is one of contrasts that magically blend into harmony. The professional, efficient wait-staff are warm and friendly; the slick functional furnishings are comfortable and relaxing and the urban colour scheme is chic yet intimate. Diners can watch chef Butters and his staff in the open kitchen creating unbelievable dishes. You might begin with creamy Crab Bisque Cappuccino served with a dollop of caviar or a terrine of Red Snapper followed by an entrée of Halibut with Basil Velouté served on a bed of Ratatouille and end with one of chef Butter's signature desserts such as Chocolate Brioche with Burnt Almond Caramel Sauce and Raspberry Compote.

1560 Water Street
Kelowna, BC V1Y 1J7
Telephone: (250) 868-8805
Open year-round • Dinner daily
Restaurateur: Audrey Surrao • Restaurateur/Executive Chef: Rodney Butters

NARAMATA HERITAGE INN & SPA

Walking onto the grounds of the Naramata Heritage Inn and Spa on the shores of beautiful Okanagan Lake is like being transported back into the mid-20th century with the benefit of today's creature comforts. Built in 1908, the inn re-opened in 2001 after being restored to its original beauty. Guests are offered accommodation in 12 luxurious, antique-furnished guestrooms.

Mediterranean-influenced cuisine is served in the formal Rock Oven Dining Room. Lunch, dinner and tapas in a more casual setting are served inside or patio-style in the Cobblestone Wine Bar and Restaurant. Both restaurants accent the fine seasonal produce and seafood of the area. The wine list features award-winning local and international selections.

3625 1st Street
Naramata, BC V0H 1N0
Telephone: (250) 496-6808 or 1-866-617-1188
E-mail: innkeeper@naramatainn.com
Web site: www.naramatainn.com
Open February to December • Lunch, dinner and tapas daily
General Managers: Janette and Norm Davies

OLD VINES PATIO
(AT QUAIL'S GATE ESTATE WINERY)

Judith Knight of Old Vines Patio has the talent to create a menu that's harmonious with the atmosphere of the location. And what a location this is — when warm breezes flow up from the shores of Okanagan Lake they intermingle with the fragrance of the vineyard.

The menu features Romaine Salad with Spicy Pecans, Gorgonzola and Roasted Garlic Vinaigrette, entrées of Coconut Curried Scallops and Prawns with vegetables and fettuccine, or Fennel crusted pork tenderloin with roasted vegetables and arugula salad. Favourite desserts include Vanilla Crème Brûlée and Triple Chocolate Cheesecake with Raspberry Coulis.

Quail's Gate Estate Winery provides the wine list. Tours of the winery are offered May to mid-October and the wine shop is open daily for tasting and sales.

3303 Boucherie Road
Kelowna, BC V1Z 2H3
Telephone: (250) 769-4451 Ext: #236 or 1-800-420-9463
E-mail: patio@quailsgate.com
Web site: www.quailsgate.com
Open May through October • Lunch and dinner daily
CEO & Proprietor: Ben Stewart
Executive Chef: Judith Knight

SALTY'S BEACH HOUSE RESTAURANT

You would expect to find Salty's Beach House Restaurant under swaying palm trees on some exotic isle. Though it's definitely located on the beach, that beach happens to be in the town of Penticton on the shores of Lake Okanagan. Owner Robert Wylie reveals his wry sense of humour as he takes patrons on a seafaring "cook's tour" of the world. Salty's offers a taste of saltier climes with its funky beach-bum decor, laid-back Caribbean music and delicious seafood.

Menu choices include an international selection of soups, salads, entrées, wood-fired pizzas and desserts, all prepared with fresh local ingredients. Menu items prefaced by a palm tree symbol indicate health-conscious dishes. Salty's, known by locals and visitors as a fun dining spot with exceptional food, is listed in Anne Hardy's *Where to Eat in Canada* restaurant guide.

Enjoy Salty's cuisine during the winter season at Salty's on the Mountain at Apex Mountain Resort, Penticton, BC.

1000 Lakeshore Drive
Penticton, BC V2A 1C1
Telephone: (250) 493-5001
Web site: www.saltysbeachouse.com
Open Feb-Dec • Lunch and dinner daily
Restaurateur: Robert Wylie

SUNSET VERANDA RESTAURANT AT SUMMERHILL ESTATE WINERY

Summerhill Estate Winery, the largest certified organic vineyard in Canada, is situated high on a steep hillside overlooking the city of Kelowna. On a clear sunny day the stunning vista from the winery's aptly named Sunset Veranda Restaurant encompasses more than 40 kilometres of Lake Okanagan. Owner Stephen Cipes's vision is "to provide the very best from pure nature for those who appreciate all natural foods and wines."

There is much to see and do at Summerhill: take a tour of the only Champagne-making facility in Canada, wonder at the Great Pyramid replica, visit the on-site Native Earth House and First Settlers' Cabin Museum, enjoy complimentary wine-tasting or browse through the gift and wine shop

Of course, it is essential that you experience lunch or dinner in the winery's restaurant during your visit. Chef Brad Wahl offers delicious soups, salads, desserts and expertly prepared entrées all designed to complement Summerhill wines. As well, the restaurant offers catered dinners for special events.

4870 Chute Lake Road
Kelowna, BC V1W 4M3
Telephone: (250) 764-8000 or 1-800-667-3538
E-mail: info@summerhill.bc.ca
Web site: www.summerhill.bc.ca
Open Feb-Dec • Lunch daily; dinner daily (summer), Tuesday to Saturday (winter)
Winemaker/Owner: Stephen Cipes • Executive Chef: Brad W. Wahl

THE TEAHOUSE RESTAURANT AT KELOWNA LAND & ORCHARD

Do not be mislead by the designation "teahouse" as this eatery is indeed a full-service restaurant featuring seating in beautifully appointed dining rooms as well as on the patio. Perched on a high ridge overlooking the city of Kelowna and surrounded by a working orchard, The Teahouse offers guests superb dining in a pastoral setting. It is truly a sunny, bright and magical location.

Guests may also visit the farm's fresh fruit market, petting zoo and a farm store that features a wide selection of local crafts, souvenirs and homemade condiments.

3002 Dunster Road
Kelowna, BC V1W 4A6
Telephone: (250) 712-9404
E-mail: klo@k-l-o.com
Web site: www.k-l-o.com
Open February 14 to December 30 • Lunch & dinner daily
Owner: Kelowna Land & Orchard Company Ltd. • Executive Chef: Chris Helmer

THE WILLIAMS INN

The Williams Inn dining rooms occupy two levels of a one-hundred-year-old home located in the heart of downtown Kelowna. Tastefully decorated, each dining room offers a choice of seating: open area, window view or intimate alcove. Owned and operated for the past fourteen years by European-trained executive chef Willi Franz and his partner Rene Haudenschild, the restaurant offers traditional European cuisine with new-world accents.

Chef Franz shapes the inn's superb menu around locally grown ingredients complemented by a wide selection of regional and international wines. Seasonal dishes may include entrees such as local Nicola Valley Venison Hunter Style or Fresh BC Salmon with Savory Hollandaise.

526 Lawrence Avenue
Kelowna, BC V1Y 6L7
Telephone: (250) 763-5136
Web site: www.thewilliamsinn.com
Open: year-round * Dinner daily * Lunch: Monday to Friday
Owner/Executive Chef: Willi Franz * Owner: Rene Haudenschild

VANCOUVER AND ENVIRONS

Celebrated as one of the world's most beautiful cities, Vancouver is a visitor's dream destination and resident's ideal home. Known as Canada's Gateway to the Pacific, the city takes pride in its international character and wealth of cultural and natural entertainment. The Vancouver dining scene is considered to be among the finest in the world, with a variety of first-class restaurants featuring traditional, ethnic, contemporary Pacific Northwest and fusion-style cuisine.

BIN 941 & BIN 942 TAPAS PARLOURS

Restaurateur and chef Gordon Martin has successfully brought to the Vancouver dining scene his upscale version of Iberian tapas dining. Tapas, or "little snacks," are traditionally served in small specialty bars. Like the atmosphere in European counterparts, BIN 941 and sister establishment BIN 942 are eclectic, social and hopping with activity.

BIN 941 and BIN 942 are extremely popular and very small, so be prepared to come early or wait in line. Each restaurant features an open kitchen with banquette-style, bar and table seating. Martin has fused traditional Old World tapas selections with his own blend of Pacific Northwest cuisine. The resulting flavours are complex, at times exotic, and always delicious. An extensive selection of wines and handcrafted beers, chosen to highlight the cuisine, are served from the bar.

BIN 941
941 Davie Street
Vancouver, BC V6Z 1B9
Telephone: (604) 683-1246
Open year-round • Monday to
Saturday: 5:00 p.m. to 2:00 a.m.
Sunday: 5:00 p.m. to midnight
Restaurateur: Gordon Martin

BIN 942
1521 West Broadway
Vancouver, BC V6J 1W6
Telephone: (604) 734-9421
Open year-round • Monday to
Friday: 5:00 p.m. to 2:00 a.m.
Saturday 5:00 p.m. to midnight • Sunday: 5:00 p.m. to 1 a.m.
Restaurateur: Gordon Martin

BISHOP'S RESTAURANT

John Bishop, the delightfully warm and friendly owner of Bishop's, describes his restaurant's culinary style as "international new food." By combining traditional European cooking techniques with the large variety of fresh international ingredients available in Vancouver markets, he and his staff are able to create fare that keeps faithful patrons coming back. Under the direction of executive chef Dennis Green, the menu is changed weekly to keep pace with the ever-changing supply of fresh local ingredients. Always included are specialties such as rack of lamb, fresh seafood and fillet of beef. All dishes are prepared on site, including fresh-baked bread, pastries and desserts.

Bishop's, with its efficient and casually elegant dining room, is located on bustling West Fourth Avenue in Kitsilano and is open daily for dinner.

2183 West Fourth Avenue
Vancouver, BC V6K 1N7
Telephone: (604) 738-2025
E-mail: inquire@bishopsonline.com
Web site: www.bishopsonline.com
Open year-round • Dinner daily
Owner: John Bishop • Executive Chef: Dennis Green

C RESTAURANT

In a few short years, Harry Kambolis has created the definitive seafood restaurant catering to avant-garde gourmet tastes. Situated on the busy waterfront at Falsecreek, C Restaurant is the epitome of modernity. The two-storey restaurant features vaulted ceilings and expansive views. Simple, chic, cool and classy all describe the ambience of C. Whether they are on the busy main level, seated in high-backed chairs surrounding tables dressed in crisp white linen or in the more intimate upstairs gallery, diners experience the cutting edge of style and cuisine.

Impeccably prepared and presented seafood is the core of the menu. There is a very small section on the luncheon and dinner menus of vegetarian and meat dishes. You may choose from several varieties of caviar at the raw seafood bar as well as a host of appetizers on the menu. A fixed price sampler menu featuring six courses plus dessert is an

excellent way to experience the true talents of chef de cuisine Rob Clarke and his kitchen staff. A comprehensive wine list features an international selection of fine wines served by the glass or bottle.

2-1600 Howe Street (on Falsecreek Waterfront)
Vancouver, BC V6Z 2L9
Telephone: (604) 681-1164
E-mail: info@crestaurant.com
Web site: www.crestaurant.com
Open year-round: Dinner daily • Lunch: Monday to Friday (Summer and Christmas season only)
Executive Chef: Rob Clark • Owner: Harry Kambolis

CIN CIN

When you dine at Cin Cin you feel all the sun-splashed warmth of the Mediterranean countryside. A spirit of mellow gaiety infuses the decor and atmosphere. The restaurant more than measures up to its quaint name, derived from chin chin, a toast meaning "to good health, old friends and the pleasures of food and wine."

Situated upstairs at 1154 Robson Street, in the heart of busy downtown Vancouver, Cin Cin offers French- and Italian-style fare augmented by premier local ingredients. Here you will find specialties from the restaurant's alder-fired oven, grill and rotisserie, such as Dijon Crusted Free-Range Chicken, Juniper Marinated Pork Chops or Pizza with House Smoked Wild Salmon. For those who prefer a meatless entrée, a comprehensive vegetarian menu is offered daily.

All baked goods are prepared on site, including an exciting variety of sumptuous desserts. As well, Cin Cin offers an extensive wine selection carefully selected to accent the cuisine.

1154 Robson Street (2nd floor)
Vancouver, BC V6E 1B5
Telephone: (604) 688-7338

Web site: www.cincin.net (web site reservations taken)
Open year-round • Lunch: Monday to Friday • Dinner: Daily • Late-night menu available
Owner: Jack Evrensel • Executive Chef: Romy Prasad

DIVA AT THE MET

Diva at the Met, located in the luxurious Metropolitan Hotel in downtown Vancouver's business district, is much more than your standard hotel restaurant. Expectations run high when you dine at Diva with its reputation for award-winning fare. You will not be disappointed: Chef Baechler and his staff ingeniously create a brand of international cuisine using British Columbian ingredients interwoven with the eclectic culinary styles of other countries. Enjoy dishes such as Salad of Spicy British Columbia Striped Prawns, Minted English Peas and Fennel, Bacon-Wrapped Ahi Tuna with Lemon, Caper, Tomato and Chive Butter Sauce or Lemon and Thyme Marinated Baby Chicken with Creamed Watercress Mashed Potatoes followed by a special Diva fruit dessert

Diva at the Met is superbly decorated in neutral shades highlighted with glass, marble and bronze to produce a natural, warm effect. A centrally located Waldorf-style open kitchen affords patrons interesting views of food preparation. The service is impeccable; the attentive, informed staff make your dining experience memorable. Diva at the Met is open for breakfast, lunch, weekend brunch, dinner and after-theatre dining.

The Metropolitan Hotel is designated an AAA four-diamond hotel and is a member of the luxury collection of Preferred Hotels and Resorts Worldwide. The hotel was originally constructed according to the ancient Chinese art of feng shui and continues in that tradition today. Hotel amenities include 197 deluxe guest rooms and suites, health club and spa, conference and private dining services, catering service and an executive business centre complete with secretarial service and all office amenities.

645 Howe Street
Vancouver, BC V6C 2Y9
Web site: www.metropolitan.com
Hotel telephone: (604) 687-1122 or 1-800-667-2300
Restaurant telephone: (604) 602-7788
E-mail restaurant reservations: reservations@divamet.com
Open year-round
Breakfast, lunch, dinner and after-theatre dining daily • Weekend brunch
Hotel Manager: Tom Waithe • Executive Chef: Scott Baechler

KIRIN MANDARIN RESTAURANT

In Vancouver, a city of refined oriental cuisine, the name Kirin is associated with high quality. Kirin Restaurant Group operates four restaurants, all of which consistently receive national and international acclaim from food critics and travel writers.

Opened in 1987, the original Kirin Mandarin Restaurant in downtown Vancouver features the northern cuisine of Beijing. Specialties include freshly prepared Dim Sum, Peking Duck and entrées prepared from live seafood. Elegant nouveau Chinese décor, with black lacquer furnishings and stunning art, provides diners with a dramatic atmosphere in keeping with the meal.

Kirin Mandarin Restaurant
#102-1166 Alberni Street
Vancouver, BC V6E 3Z3
Telephone: (604) 682-8833
E-mail: info@kirinrestaurant.com
Web site: www.kirinrestaurant.com
Open year-round: Lunch and Dinner daily
Proprietors: Kirin Restaurant Group

LE CROCODILE

Vancouver is a city with sophisticated tastes. Diners know what they like and how it should be prepared. It is evident that owner and chef Michel Jacob must be preparing his Alsace-style French cuisine perfectly at Le Crocodile for he

has remained high on diners' and critics' lists since the restaurant's inception in 1983. Chef Jacob and his staff take pride in using authentic French culinary techniques to create all their own stocks, sauces and accompaniments from the finest products available.

In stylishly elegant surroundings, you will be served traditional French dishes such as Alsacian-Style Onion Tart and Curly Endive Salad, Pan-Fried Dover Sole with Beurre Noisette and Capers, and French Lemon Tart. The fine selection of wines and spirits were chosen to enhance the menu.

100-909 Burrard Street (entrance on Smithe)
Vancouver, BC V6Z 2N2
Telephone: (604) 669-4298
E-mail: lecrocodile@telus.net
Open year-round • Lunch: Monday to Friday • Dinner: Monday to Saturday
Closed Sunday and holidays • Owner and Chef: Michel Jacob

L'EMOTION RESTAURANT

Minna and Jean-Yves Benoit took a chance and opened their restaurant in residential West Vancouver away from the mainstream dining areas of the city. It may take a little extra time to get there but your effort will be greatly rewarded with Jean-Yvés' wonderful southern French cuisine and Minna's warm hospitality.

The restaurant is decorated in a warm French-country style with original artwork gracing the walls. Diners are presented with a menu that changes frequently to accommodate the best ingredients of each season. Expect to find fare such as Fresh Crab Mousse with Green Bean Salad, Avocado and Tomato Confit, Creamy Celeriac Soup with Alba Truffle Oil, Braised Local Lamb with Thyme Ratatouille Provençale followed by Sweet L'Emotion desserts. Bon Appetit!

4368 Marine Drive
West Vancouver, BC V7V 1P1
Telephone: (604) 926-1063

E-mail: mbenoit@axion.net
Web site: www.lemotion.com
Open year-round • Dinner: Wednesday to Sunday
Co-owner: Jean-Yves Benoit and Minna • Executive Chef: Jean-Yves Benoit

LUMIÈRE RESTAURANT

It may be said that chef Robert Feenie's meteoric rise in culinary circles can be found in his ability to express a feeling of complexity through simplicity. This expression not only applies to his culinary style but is also carried through in the décor and ambience of his restaurant. Under his hand common ingredients are transformed into artfully presented taste sensations. Entrees such as Scallop Carpaccio with Jalapeno, Mint and Cilantro or Lamb Chop with Summer Succotash, Lamb Reduction and Basil Oil or dessert like Figs and Apricots Baked with Oranges, served with a Japanese Plum Wine Sabayon, are examples of fare to be found on the menu.

In a city known for its exceptional cuisine it is noteworthy that Lumière Restaurant has been awarded *Vancouver Magazine's* Best Restaurant and Best French Restaurant awards for the past six years. Chef Feenie has written the cookbook, *Rob Feenie Cooks at Lumière,* and is also featured on the Food Network in a series titled *New Classics with Chef Rob Feenie.* He is truly a remarkable chef with a remarkable restaurant!

2551 West Broadway
Vancouver, BC V6K 2E9
Telephone: (604) 739-8185
E-mail: lumiere@relaischateaux.com
Web site: www.lumiere.ca
Open year-round • Dinner: from 5:30 pm (closed Monday)
Owner and Executive Chef: Robert Feenie • General Manager: Mark Steenge

MEMPHIS BLUES BARBECUE HOUSE

Southern grits and fried pickles may not make the culinary transition from the mid-south to Vancouver but Memphis-style barbecue is a universal hit. Keep in mind that in the South "barbecue" is not a verb but a noun that refers to a succulent meal of smoked pork, coleslaw, cornbread and spicy beans. Owners George Sui and Park Heffelfinger travelled throughout Tennessee to find "the best barbecue flavour" and serve it up at two Vancouver locations.

Vancouver Magazine's 14th Annual Restaurant Awards gave Memphis Blues Barbecue House a coveted "Gold" in the "Best Meat" category. As both customers and food critics give rave reviews to owners Siu and Heffelfinger, make sure you come early to avoid disappointment. The restaurant also offers catering and take-out menus.

1465 West Broadway
Vancouver, BC V6L 1H6
Telephone: (604) 738-6806
&
1342 Commercial Drive
Vancouver, BC V5L 3X6
Telephone: (604) 215-2599
E-mail: dgsiu@telus.net
Open year-round • Lunch and dinner daily
Owners: George Siu & Park Heffelfinger

RAINCITY GRILL

When owner Harry Kambolis opened Raincity Grill in 1992 his aim was to give patrons a total Vancouver dining experience, hence the appropriate tongue-in-cheek name in a city that prides itself on its mild, albeit wet, climate.

Located in Vancouver's West End and overlooking the busy activities at English Bay Beach, Raincity Grill offers fine fare created almost exclusively with Pacific Northwest ingredients. Believing in the superior quality of the area's produce, meats and seafood it has become the restaurant's mission to, as owner Kambolis put it, "support producers who practice the sustainability of food resources indigenous to our region." Under the watchful eye of executive chef Sean Cousins, diners can expect creative dishes such as Dungeness Crab and Filbert Cake with currant emulsion, grilled watermelon and bitter greens, Grand Fir-Glazed BC Trout with goat cheese stuffing, candy-striped beets, potato dumplings and brown butter followed by Okanagan Cherry Torte. The wine cellar is stocked exclusively with vintages from British Columbia, Washington State, Oregon and California chosen to complement their Pacific Northwest cuisine.

1193 Denman Street
Vancouver, BC V6G 2N1
Telephone: (604) 685-7337
E-mail: info@raincitygrill.com
Web site: www.raincitygrill.com

Open year-round • Dinner daily from 5:00 p.m.
Brunch: Saturday and Sunday 10:30 a.m. to 2:30 p.m.
Owner: Harry Kambolis • Manager/Sommelier: Brent Hayman • Executive Chef: Sean Cousins

SEASONS RESTAURANT IN QUEEN ELIZABETH PARK

Seasons Restaurant is situated in Queen Elizabeth Park on a knoll that is the highest promontory within Vancouver's city limits. Reclaimed from two spent rock quarries, the park, with its beautiful gardens and streams, is a tribute to the environmental consciousness of British Columbians. With its expansive windows and skylights, Seasons Restaurant offers diners an atmosphere of airy brightness that is complementary to the park-like surroundings. During the day, diners delight in a stunning vista of manicured gardens and parkland spreading out to the big city skyline and mountains beyond. At night, candle-lit tables

sparkle in competition with the lights of the city below. The decor is comfortable and relaxing, with neutral-coloured woods, crisp white linens and greenery.

Executive chef Lynda Larouche prepares Pacific Northwest cuisine enhanced by regional ingredients. Menu highlights may include Mixed Baby Lettuces with roast pine nuts and snow goat cheese, Smoked Alaskan Black Cod with Grainy Mustard Beurre Blanc, a vegetarian entrée of Curried Lentils Baked in Phyllo followed by the restaurant's signature Sunburnt Lemon Pie.

Little Mountain in Queen Elizabeth Park
Cambie Street at 33rd Avenue
Vancouver, BC
Telephone: (604) 874-8008 or 1-800-632-9422
E-mail: info@vancouverdine.com
Web site: www.vancouverdine.com
Open year-round • Lunch, dinner and weekend brunch
Manager: Sue Carlisle • Executive Chef: Lynda Larouche

SIMPLY THAI

Simply Thai is found in the heart of Yaletown, a reclaimed warehouse area of Vancouver filled with stylish shops and eateries. The small to medium-sized restaurant with its warm creamy-yellow walls, flowing arches and southeast Asian artwork was designed to exude the warm tropical feeling of southern Thailand in a fresh upscale fashion. From the entrance a curved aisle carries through the restaurant accessing two levels of seating and a very small bar which overlooks the open kitchen.

Chef and owner Siriwan "Grace" Rerksuttisiridach and her staff prepare authentic Thai cuisine that may well turn customers into Spring Roll and Pad Thai addicts. Customers may choose the heat intensity of individual dishes by selecting a range of one to four chilies on the menu. Try dishes such as Som Tum, a green papaya salad made with fresh lime juice, tomatoes, peanuts and fresh greens; Chicken Swimming Angels, a creation of sliced chicken served on a bed of fresh cooked spinach and topped with homemade peanut sauce; or Goong Nam-prig Paow with its sautéed prawns in sweet chili sauce served with seasonal vegetables and fresh Thai basil.

1211 Hamilton Street
Vancouver, BC V6B 6K3
Telephone: (604) 642-0123
E-mail: info@simplythairestaurant.com
Web site: www.simplythairestaurant.com
Open year-round • Lunch: Monday to Friday • Dinner: Monday to Sunday
Take-out available
Executive Chef/Owner: Siriwan (Grace) Rerksuttisiridach

THE TEAHOUSE RESTAURANT IN STANLEY PARK

When you ask a Vancouverite to name the most important feature of the city, the answer is likely to be Stanley Park. Queen Victoria's Canadian representative, Lord Stanley, dedicated this 1,000-acre natural wonderland in 1889. A seawall open for jogging, in-line skating, walking and biking, offers spectacular views of the North Shore mountains, Burrard Inlet, English Bay and the Gulf Islands. Stroll a myriad of winding paths amid lush flora and towering Douglas fir or, if less energetic, take a horse-drawn carriage or bus tour. Also located within the park are the Vancouver Aquarium and Marine Science Centre, Lost Lagoon, a Children's Zoo, rose gardens, beaches and numerous picnic areas.

There is no doubt that The Teahouse Restaurant is situated in one of the most enviable locations in Vancouver. Originally a Second World War garrison and officers' mess, the restaurant is nestled under a canopy of enormous Douglas fir trees, surrounded by manicured gardens and

blessed with a view that one can imagine leads to the Orient.

The chefs prepare a style of contemporary West Coast cuisine that takes full advantage of the wide variety of ingredients available. Entrée specialties include Salmon Tournedos, Sterling Silver New York Steak and Wok-fried Asian Vegetables and Crispy Tofu.

The Teahouse Restaurant in Stanley Park is consistently rated one of Vancouver's top restaurants, with recognition from *Gourmet, Vancouver Magazine, Zagat Survey-Vancouver Restaurants* and *Fodor's Vancouver Guide*.

7501 Stanley Park Drive
Ferguson Point in Stanley Park
Vancouver, BC V6G 3E2
Telephone: (604) 669-3281 or 1-800-280-9893
E-mail: info@vancouverdine.com
Web site: www.vancouverdine.com
Open year-round • Lunch, dinner and weekend brunch
Executive Chef: Shayne Shepherd

TOJO'S RESTAURANT

Tojo's Restaurant may be tucked away on the second floor of a modern office tower on West Broadway but the restaurant is anything but ordinary. In fact, in a city with very high Japanese culinary standards, Tojo's is known to be one of the best. It is a tribute to Hidekazu Tojo's talent and success that he is as highly regarded by peers in the food industry as he is by his patrons.

The restaurant is tranquilly decorated in traditional Japanese style. Seated at the sushi bar, customers can focus on the intricate art form of sushi preparation and presentation; seated at a table, customers can enjoy a spectacular view of the city and North Shore mountains.

Consistently rated by travel and dining publications as one of Vancouver's best restaurants, Tojo's is a must for earnest Japanese cuisine lovers. Choose from the à la carte menu or "trust-the-chef" and dine Omakase style: specify the price and let the chefs present you with their choice from the kitchen.

#202-777 West Broadway
Vancouver, BC V5Z 4J7
Telephone: (604) 872-8050; 872-5051
E-mail: info@tojos.com
Web site: www.tojos.com (web site reservations taken)
Open year-round • Dinner: Monday to Saturday
Owner/Executive Chef: Hidekazu Tojo

UMBERTO MENGHI'S VANCOUVER RESTAURANTS
Including
CIRCOLO
IL GIARDINO AND UMBERTO'S

Owner Umberto Menghi divides his time between his five acclaimed Vancouver and Whistler area restaurants and his Villa Delia Cooking School in the beautiful, rolling hills of Tuscany. Each of his restaurants feature a slightly different ambience, and five of them offer unique menus. All can be counted on to provide a memorable meal of fine food, fine wine and superb service.

CIRCOLO

Circolo, Umberto Menghi's newest restaurant, breaks from the traditional Italian cuisine prepared in his other establishments. Situated in the trendy Yaletown area of downtown Vancouver, Circolo highlights the cuisine of Menghi's three favourite cities:

Florence, Paris and New York.

"Circolo" translates from the Italian as "a place where people meet and socialize." In this atmosphere the restaurant invites you to relax, converse with friends and enjoy a repast of fine food and drink.

1116 Mainland Street
Vancouver, BC V6B 2T9
Telephone: (604) 687-1116
Web site: www.umberto.com
Open year-round • Dinner: Monday to Saturday

IL GIARDINO AND UMBERTO'S

Il Giardino and Umberto Menghi's original restaurant, Umberto's, maintain separate exteriors but are accessible to each other on the inside and share a common kitchen and menu. Umberto's, the smaller of the two establishments, offers dining for small groups, while Il Giardino, designed after a Tuscan home, offers seating in the main dining room and patio.

The extensive menu and wonderful aromas wafting from the kitchen make decisions almost unbearable. Will you sample Carousel of Antipasti, savour Grilled Assorted Mushrooms and Roasted Garlic, or sup on traditional Minestrone Vegetable Soup? Will you try pasta such as Cannelloni filled with Game Meats or choose an entrée such as Ossobuco Milanese with Saffron Risotto? Whatever you decide you will not be disappointed.

1382 Hornby Street
Vancouver, BC V6Z 1W5
Telephone: (604) 669-2422
Web site: www.umberto.com
Open year-round • Lunch: Monday to Friday • Dinner: Monday to Saturday

VICTORIA AND THE GULF ISLANDS

You are never very far from the ocean and a relaxed pace of life when you are in Victoria and the islands. The area is blessed with a mild climate, great beauty and abundant natural and cultural activities. Here you can expect excellent cuisine and genuine hospitality.

THE AERIE RESORT

Eagles always build their aeries (nests) on the highest possible vantage point to keep a sharp eye on prey and predators. With this in mind, it is hard to imagine a more appropriate name for The Aerie Resort, perched high upon a mountainside overlooking Finlayson Arm, only a thirty-minute drive from the city of Victoria. Opened in 1991, the Aerie Resort is a member of the elite international hotel association Relais & Châteaux, holder of both the AAA Four Diamond Award and the Mobil Four Star Award, as well as a member of the prestigious dining associations Chaîne des Rotisseurs and Confrérie du Sabre d'Or.

The Aerie offers all the amenities of a world-class luxury resort, including an Aveda Beauty and Wellness Centre, full-service meeting facility for small- to medium-size groups, indoor roof-top pool, hot tub and sauna, outdoor hot tub and tennis court. Available nearby are a wealth of outdoor activities, including golf, kayaking, hiking, bird watching and sailing. Management will also arrange cultural, historical and winery tours for guests. Accommodation with breakfast is offered in 29 elegantly appointed hotel rooms and suites, many with private balconies, Jacuzzis and fireplaces.

The restaurant, under the direction of chef de cuisine Christophe Letard, offers resort guests and the public classic French-style cuisine showcasing Vancouver Island ingredients. At the Aerie recipes are never static for staff change and suit their dishes to highlight local seasonal ingredients.

600 Ebedora Lane
Malahat, BC V0R 2L0
Telephone: (250) 743-7115 or 1-800-518-1933
E-mail: resort@aerie.bc.ca
Web site: www.aerie.bc.ca
Open year-round • Lunch and dinner daily (breakfast daily — only available to resident guests)
Owner/General Manager: Maria Schuster • Executive Chef: Christophe Letard

CAFE BRIO

Owners Silvia Marcolini and Greg Hays combined their talents to create a perfect dining experience for food connoisseurs. Their attention to service, décor and food and beverages has brought numerous awards and praise to Cafe Brio.

The interior is reminiscent of a Mediterranean bistro. Ceramic tiles, mellow woods and aged wrought iron warmed with colours of earthy yellow and burnt sienna glow with light from the windows, skylights and unique lighting fixtures.

Savour dishes such as Hearts of Romaine freshly presented with lemon pepper dressing and shaved Parmesan cheese, Cobble Hill Free-Range Chicken Breast served with braised greens, roast shallots, tomato confit, crispy polenta and lemon thyme jus followed by Chocolate Hazelnut Souffle Cake with Burnt Orange Red Wine Ice Cream. Whenever possible, all dishes are created with fresh, local, certified-organic products.

944 Fort Street
Victoria, BC V8V 3K2
Telephone: (250) 383-0009 or 1-866-270-5461
E-mail: reservations@cafe-brio.com
Web site: www.cafe-brio.com
Open year-round • Dinner daily
Restaurateurs: Silvia Marcolini and Greg Hays • Chef: Chris Dignan

CAMILLE'S RESTAURANT

Camille's Restaurant is situated on Bastion Square in the heart of old downtown Victoria. Located below street level, the dining room creates a dark, comfortable and romantic ambience. The menu is diverse, with seasonal offerings that highlight ingredients from the restauranteurs' personal network of independent farmers and growers. Fiddlehead ferns, wild salmon, pheasant, chanterelle and morel mushrooms, red gooseberries and winter sorrel will all find a place on the menu as the seasons change.

Restaurateurs David Mincey and Paige Robinson have surrounded themselves with warm, knowledgeable staff who treat new and returning customers with a high level of service.

45 Bastion Square
Victoria, BC V8W 1J1
Telephone: (250) 381-3433
E-mail: info@camillesrestaurant.com
Web site: www.camillesrestaurant.com
Open year-round • Dinner Tuesday to Sunday
Restaurateurs: David Mincey and Paige Robinson • Chef: Chris Hammer

FAIRMONT EMPRESS
Including
THE EMPRESS ROOM
THE BENGAL LOUNGE
KIPLING'S
AFTERNOON TEA

It is impossible to think of Victoria without conjuring up pictures of The Fairmont Empress, the "grande dame" of hotels. Located in the heart of British Columbia's capital city, The Empress has been standing guard over the inner harbour since its doors opened in 1908. Part of the original Canadian Pacific transportation dynasty, The Empress would greet guests recently disembarked from the Orient on Canadian Pacific steamships or who had made the arduous journey from Eastern Canada by rail. Today the mode of transportation may be different but the destination is the

same. The Empress continues to offer guests the grandeur and elegance of a bygone era supplemented with today's modern amenities. In fact, The Empress has been included in *Condé Nast Traveler* magazine's list of top 500 hotels, resorts, spas and cruise lines.

Hotel features include 476 guestrooms and suites, two restaurants, a lounge, convention facilities and daily afternoon tea. Health and fitness aficionados will appreciate the new 8,000 square foot Willow Stream Spa.

The Empress Dining Room features candle-lit dining in a relaxing atmosphere of luxury. It offers contemporary British Columbia cuisine that highlights the freshest seasonal products available. The restaurant has an award-winning wine list, featuring many local varieties, and an exceptional dessert selection from their internationally renowned pastry team.

The Bengal Lounge offers à la carte dining as well as its famous curry buffet luncheon. The curry buffet tradition is a historical carry-over from the early days of The Empress and her Indo-Pacific British Commonwealth ties.

Kipling's, named after Rudyard Kipling who was a frequent visitor to Victoria, offers a casual all-day buffet and à la carte menu. Sunday brunch remains popular.

No one should visit Victoria without partaking of the queenly Victorian tradition of Afternoon Tea at The Fairmont Empress. Perfectly brewed tea, poured from silver teapots, accompanies dainty tea sandwiches, pastries, fresh berries, warm scones, toasted crumpets and heavy Jersey cream. Queen Victoria herself would be right at home ordering a spot of tea!

721 Government Street
Victoria, BC V8W 1W5
Telephone: (250) 384-8111 or 1-800-441-1414
E-mail: theempress@fairmont.com
Web site: www.fairmont.com
Open year-round • Breakfast, lunch, afternoon tea and dinner daily
General Manager: Ian Powell • Executive Chef: Takashi Ito

HASTINGS HOUSE

This 30-acre estate is located on beautiful Salt Spring Island, the largest and most populated of the Gulf Islands. The island is accessible by plane or boat. Daily ferry service to Salt Spring Island operates from three terminals: Tsawwassen, just south of Vancouver; Swartz Bay, near Victoria; and Crofton, near Duncan on Vancouver Island.

Hastings House, a member of the prestigious hotel association Relais & Châteaux, offers guests superior accommodation in a peaceful, serene setting. Located in six different restored buildings, the inn has 16 suites and two cottages, all individually decorated to express their own personal charm.

Under the direction of executive chef Marcel Kauer, guests are served gourmet cuisine featuring fresh produce from the fields, waters and gardens of the islands. In the words of the owners, "Hastings House strives to make each and every guest feel they have been invited to the home of a friend."

160 Upper Ganges Road
Salt Spring Island, BC V8K 2S2
Telephone: (250) 537-2362 or 1-800-661-9255
E-mail: info@hastingshouse.com
Web site: www.hastingshouse.com
Open year-round
Breakfast and Afternoon Tea for inn guests, dinner daily • Reservations required for public dining
Manager: Shirley McLaughlin • Executive Chef and Manager: Marcel Kauer

HERALD STREET CAFFE

Since opening in 1982, the Herald Street Caffe has become the focal point for consistently fine dining in Victoria. Partners Paul Bell and Geoff Radons work diligently to maintain a reputation for impeccable service and fare that exceeds the norm. For its wine service, the restaurant was awarded the *Decanter Magazine*/Robert Mondavi "Wine by the Glass" international Grand Award and the Award of Excellence from *Wine Spectator Magazine*.

The restaurant is casually elegant with a semi-open design concept featuring mellow golden hues accented with impressive artwork and floral arrangements. The linen-covered tables are set with sparkling tableware.

Guests have a difficult time choosing from the outstanding items on the menu which may include crêpes filled with local wild chanterelle mushrooms, slow roasted orange and vanilla-scented duck and a host of wonderful homemade soups, salads and pastas. As well, all the breads, baked goods and delicious desserts are made on the premises. You are well advised to book early for reservations so as not to be disappointed.

546 Herald Street
Victoria, BC V8W 1S6
Telephone: (250) 381-1441
E-mail: wecan@shaw.ca
Web site: www.café-brio.com/dining/HeraldStreetCaffe.htm
Open year-round • Dinner daily • Lunch: Wednesday to Saturday • Sunday brunch
Owners: Paul & Angelika Bell
     Jennifer & Geoff Radons
Executive Chef: Geoff Redons

J & J WONTON NOODLE HOUSE

Chefs in the Vancouver Island Region say that J & J Noodle House is a restaurant that must not be missed — testament to chef Joseph Wong's expertise. Simply put, the establishment is known as the best place for Chinese cuisine.

Located in downtown Victoria amid the shops of Antique Row, the restaurant offers diners traditionally prepared Cantonese and Szechuan cuisine with the frequent addition of nontraditional fresh local ingredients. A glassed-in open kitchen allows full viewing of the busy staff as they prepare a variety of noodle dishes, soups and entrées such as Beef Hot Pot, Imperial Prawns with Spicy Garlic Wine Sauce or Szechuan-style Rack of Lamb.

1012 Fort Street
Victoria, BC V8V 3K4
Telephone: (250) 383-0680
E-mail: jjnoodle@telus.net
Web site: www.jjnoodlehouse.com
Open year-round • Lunch and dinner: Tuesday to Saturday • Take-out available
Owner/Chef: Joseph Wong

KINGFISHER OCEANSIDE RESTAURANT AT KINGFISHER OCEANSIDE RESORT & SPA

It is absolutely imperative that when a restaurant occupies a particular site, such as the Kingfisher Oceanside Restaurant does, it specialize in seafood. The magnificent view, seen from the restaurant's windows overlooking Georgia Strait, is simply stunning. Diners are frequently entertained with sights of bald eagles, indigenous marine wildlife, Alaska-bound cruise liners, fishing boats and white furled sailboats parading across the watery horizon. The menu features fresh seafood including locally harvested Fanny Bay oysters, meat and vegetarian entrées as well as a fine selection of soups, salads and desserts.

The resort offers a variety of accommodation choices ranging from beachfront suites and apartments to lodge-style hotel rooms. The resort operates a full service spa featuring facials and other beauty treatments, massage, aromatherapy, hydrotherapy and reflexology.

4330 Island Highway South
Royston, BC V9N 9R9
Telephone: (250) 338-1323 or 1-800-663-7929
E-mail: info@kingfisherspa.com
Web site: www.kingfisherspa.com
Open year-round • Breakfast, lunch and dinner daily
Owner: Lucas Stiefvater • Executive Chef: Ronald St. Pierre • Sous Chef: David Prevost

THE MAHLE HOUSE RESTAURANT

Brother and sister partners Maureen Loucks and Delbert Horrocks have been successfully operating The Mahle House Restaurant in the little village of Cedar, a ten-minute drive south of Nanaimo, for the past 20 years. Horrocks is the wine expert, selecting perfect wines to complement chef Loucks's wonderful food.

The house, built in 1904 and painted an unusual yet appealing orange colour, invites you turn and enter the driveway. Stroll through the enclosed English-style garden or take a peek at the organic kitchen garden to see what ripe gourmet vegetables will be accompanying your evening meal. Step inside and you will find décor that is casually elegant in a relaxed country setting.

Loucks prepares dishes from a menu that changes weekly to take advantage of the freshest products from the local area. She says the rabbit, free-range chicken and venison come from down the road, while most of the herbs and vegetables come from her own garden. Her enthusiasm for fine cuisine is clearly evident in her preparation of recipes such as Smoked Gouda Cheese Soup, Braised Rabbit with Wild Mushrooms, Fresh Herbs and Mascarpone Cheese Polenta, and her Vegetarian Plate of roast garlic and goat cheese, mashed potatoes with grilled peppers, mushrooms, eggplant and zucchini on an Italian tomato sauce. It is essential that you leave room for dessert, especially if the White Chocolate Crème Brûlée and Boca Negra are on the menu.

2104 Hemer Road
Nanaimo, BC V9X 1L8
Telephone: (250) 722-3621
E-mail: info@mahlehouse.com
Web site: www.mahlehouse.com
Open year-round • Dinner: Wednesday to Sunday (reservations appreciated)
Owners: Maureen Loucks and Delbert Horrocks
Chef: Maureen Loucks

THE OLD HOUSE RESTAURANT

The Old House Restaurant is situated on the banks of the Courtenay River within the town of Courtenay in the lovely Comox Valley. This central region of Vancouver Island is blessed with an abundance of natural beauty that ranges from the high alpine areas of Mount Washington and the Forbidden Plateau down through rich farmland to the ocean shoreline.

Since The Old House Restaurant opened its doors in 1974, it has been the dining establishment of choice for local residents and visitors. The restaurant is surrounded with beautifully manicured gardens and lush green lawns that border the flowing river. Inside, you will be seated in one of four dining rooms with rough-hewn timbered walls, beamed ceilings and large stone fireplaces that exude an ambience of rustic warmth and charm. In summer, dining is also available on the patio.

The menu offers a variety of homemade West Coast dishes, including an extensive selection of steak and seafood. At the on-site bakery fresh bread and tantalizing desserts are prepared daily.

1760 Riverside Lane
Courtenay, BC V9N 8C6
Telephone: (250) 338-5406
E-mail: kevin.2tomatoes@shaw.ca
Open year-round • Lunch and dinner daily
Restaurateur: Kevin Muir • Chef: Edward White

RAINCOAST CAFÉ

You only have to dine once at the RainCoast Café to realize that the staff live up to their motto: "We take pride in everything we do." This informal little bistro in the village of Tofino, on the west coast of Vancouver Island, catches your attention the moment you cross the threshold. The decor is bright and airy, with bold artwork dominating one wall and eclectic music filling the air. An open kitchen offers views of food preparation complete with tantalizing aromas.

RainCoast Café offers diners contemporary Pacific Coast cuisine fused with hints of international flavours. The staff use only the best and freshest ingredients available, offering a variety of daily specials in addition to the standard menu, with special emphasis on unique vegetarian and vegan dishes.

The restaurant has been receiving positive attention from food connoisseurs and critics for innovative fare such as the comprehensive appetizer Thai Crab Cakes with Daikon Raita, Pickled Cucumber and Napa Cabbage Slaw, the vegetarian entrée Mediterranean Portobello Tier with Salsa Verde and Lemon Garlic Vinaigrette and an Asian-style Indonesian Sweet Potato, Peanut and Coconut Soup. Award-winning British Columbian wines and micro-brewed beers are available to accompany your meal.

#101, 120 Fourth Street
Tofino, BC V0R 2Z0
Telephone: (250) 725-2215
E-mail: raincafe@island.net
Web site: www.raincoastcafe.com
Open year-round • Dinner daily (reservations recommended)
Chef/Owner: Lisa Henderson • Manager/Owner: Larry Nicolay

REBAR MODERN FOOD

If you love pick-me-up-flavour, you'll love dining at rebar modern food located in Victoria's historic Bastion Square. This corner restaurant is possibly one of the busiest in the city; the crowds being a true indicator of customer satisfaction. Rebar's philosophy to serve organic, vegetarian and creative food in a funky atmosphere is evident in selections such as shitake-tofu potstickers, a gado gado salad of seasonal vegetables with sesame-soy baked tofu and Indonesian peanut-coconut sauce or yam and pepita quesadillas. Combine your fare with an amazing variety of fruit, vegetable and combo juices, smoothies, power tonics and wheatgrass drinks and you have a libation for every taste.

All the wonderful breads, cakes and pies served at rebar are baked daily at Cascadia Wholefoods Bakery. The bakery, located at 1812 Government Street, is owned and operated by rebar's Audrey Alsterberg and features hand-shaped breads, muffins, pastries, specialty cakes and fresh fruit pies. The bakery also offers homemade soups, panini sandwiches and espresso coffee.

50 Bastion Square
Victoria, BC V8W 1J2
Telephone: (250) 361-9223
E-mail: audreydale@shaw.ca
Web site: www.rebarmodernfood.com
Open year-round • Breakfast, lunch and dinner daily
Restaurateur: Audrey Alsterberg • Chef: Wanda Urbanowicz

SHOAL HARBOUR INN AND LATCH DINING ROOMS

Guests at Shoal Harbour Inn and Latch Dining Rooms are treated to modern day amenities tastefully harmonized in traditional Vancouver Island style. The new Shoal Harbour Inn features modern five-star suites that complement the original Latch Heritage Mansion's five historic guest suites, which are decorated with custom Canadian furnishings and original artwork.

The original estate was built in the early 1900s as a private summer retreat for Walter Nichol, a wealthy Vancouver publisher and the Lieutenant-Governor of British Columbia from 1920 to 1926. Nichol requested that his architect build him a residence that utilized British Columbian wood wherever possible. The result is an impressive rustic structure, sided with bark-covered slabs of Douglas fir and tree-trunk constructed balconies and porches. The interior features expansive wood decoration with paneled walls, wood trim and hand-carved railings. It is no wonder that the building, nearly a hundred years later, remains strong and steadfast.

The Latch Dining Rooms are open to the public for lunch and dinner daily. Overnight guests are served breakfast. The restaurant uses Pacific Coast ingredients prepared in a European style.

2328 Harbour Road
Sidney, BC V8L 2P8
Telephone: (250) 656-6622 or 1-877-956-6622
E-mail: info@shoalharbourinn.com
Web site: www.shoalharbourinn.com
Open year-round • Continental breakfast for inn guests • Lunch and dinner daily
Innkeepers: Judi Ganner and Jason Fitzgerald
Dining Room Management: Katie and Irene Knowland

SOOKE HARBOUR HOUSE

Each morning when Sinclair Philip strolls through his gardens or looks shoreward to the ocean, delightful challenges greet him. What bounty from the sea will be harvested at its prime and which of the numerous varieties of vegetables, herbs, flowers and fruits are ready to be converted into fare for guests?

Sooke Harbour House has been garnering well-deserved national and international culinary awards and acclaim for many years. Seafood, often exotic, is emphasized in entrées that may feature sea cucumber, wolf eel, pink singing scallops, crab, shrimp — the list is as long as the edible species found in local waters. Other meat and vegetarian entrées

receive equal attention from the kitchen. As well, there is an ever-changing variety of appetizers, soups, salads and desserts. Dining at the inn is truly an experience that will remain etched in your fondest memories.

The inn features 28 luxury rooms and suites, most with views of the Strait of Juan de Fuca and distant snow-capped Olympic Mountains. Each suite is named for its location. The Chef's Study, dedicated to culinary lovers, overlooks the gardens and is decorated with food lovers' memorabilia. Three rooms at the top of the inn, known as The Bird's Nest, have stellar views of the ocean that ordinarily only a bird would see. All suites feature a wood-burning fireplace, comfortable sitting area and balcony or terrace. Breakfast is included in the room rates.

1528 Whiffen Spit Road
Sooke, BC V0S 1N0
Telephone: (250) 642-3421
E-mail: info@sookeharbourhouse.com
Web site: www.sookeharbourhouse.com
Open February to December (check for seasonal closure December–February)
• Breakfast for inn guests • Dinner daily
Innkeepers: Frederique and Sinclair Philip

SPINNAKERS BREWPUB & GUESTHOUSE

Spinnakers Brewpub & Guesthouse, which invites you to "drop down to the pub for a pint of ...", fits in perfectly with Victoria's British-style atmosphere. The pub is located on the waterfront and with its expansive bank of windows, provides diners with an ever-changing view of harbour activity. It is difficult to focus your attention on the meal what with curious seals, float planes, water taxis, shore birds and an occasional canoe passing by.

Spinnakers, established in 1984, is the oldest craft brewery in British Columbia and produces a wide variety of natural lagers and conventional ales for its patrons. The brewpub features a traditional taproom for socializing, and the multi-level restaurant serves pub fare and contemporary West Coast cuisine. Many of the dishes, including Hot and

Sour Soup and Spinnakers' Raspberry Vinaigrette with Mixed Greens, feature either Spinnakers' ales or malt vinegar in the recipe.

Accommodation, for adults only, is located at two sites: the 1884 Heritage Guesthouse features five antique-decorated, luxury rooms and the Garden Suites offers four suites decorated in a contemporary fashion with Asian highlights. Complimentary breakfast is served at Spinnakers.

308 Catherine Street
Victoria, BC V9A 3S8
Restaurant reservations: (250) 386-2739
Guesthouse reservations: (250) 384-2739
E-mail: spinnakers@spinnakers.com
Web site: www.spinnakers.com
Open year-round • Breakfast, lunch and dinner daily
Owner: Paul Hadfield

THE WICKANINNISH INN AND POINTE RESTAURANT

Spending a few days at The Wickaninnish Inn in Tofino is a humbling back-to-nature experience. In summer, the sun shines and sparkles off the cold blue water; in winter, Pacific storms pound wild surf over the rocks. All seasons bring their own special beauty to Tofino.

Situated on a point of land at the end of Chesterman Beach, the inn is surrounded on three sides by ocean. A giant old-growth forest backs the fourth side. Wickaninnish offers 46 guestrooms and suites, all with ocean views and private balconies. The decor is natural and rustic, with furniture created from recycled old-growth red cedar, fir or driftwood. Amenities include a full-service spa, conference and banquet facilities and a gourmet restaurant.

The Pointe Restaurant offers innovative West Coast cuisine under the direction of chef de cuisine Jim Garraway. The menu highlights fresh coastal seafood, local farm-fresh ingredients and an excellent selection of international and British Columbia wines.

Osprey Lane at Chesterman Beach
P.O. Box 250
Tofino, BC V0R 2Z0
Telephone: (250) 725-3100 or 1-800-333-4604
E-mail: pointe@wickinn.com
Web site: www.wickinn.com
Open year-round • Breakfast, lunch and dinner daily
Manager: Charles McDiarmid • Chef de Cuisine: Jim Garraway

WHISTLER RESORT AREA

It is said that a region is defined by its cuisine. How true of the Whistler resort area, for not only is the scenery magnificent, the cuisine is also. Whistler is renowned as a world-class winter and summer sports mecca, and what better way to cap off a day of fun in the mountains than to sit down to a fine meal in a world-class restaurant.

ARAXI

Araxi, named for owner Jack Evrensel's wife, has been a mainstay of Whistler's culinary scene for nearly two decades. This classy restaurant, winner of numerous national and international food and wine accolades under the guidance of executive chef Scott Kidd, features the partnering of classic French and Italian cooking techniques with regional Pacific Northwest products. The result is an epicurean delight of fine food expertly prepared and served.

Newly renovated, the restaurant features a 140-seat main dining room, lounge area, separate wine room for group dining, and outdoor summer patio and bar. The atmosphere is contemporary and chic, with mellow colours, impressive artwork and subtle romantic lighting. If you want to view the talents of Araxi's chefs, ask for a seat near the open kitchen, considerably buffered for noise with beveled-glass surrounds. Guests may choose from an extensive liquor selection and wine list featuring more than 13,000 bottles. Fifteen hundred of the bottles are kept on display in the 63° F wine refrigerator in the lounge.

Chef Scott keeps Araxi on the leading edge of dining excellence with his close attention to detail and pursuit of fine ingredients. Only the best products are used in the restaurant; fresh seafood is brought in daily from Vancouver, regional meat is used when possible, and local farmers provide cheeses, seasonal herbs, fruits and vegetables.

4222 Village Square
Whistler, BC V0N 1B4
Telephone: (604) 932-4540
E-mail: info@araxi.com
Web site: www.araxi.com (web site reservations taken)
Open year-round • Dinner daily • Lunch daily in summer
Owner: Jack Evrensel • Executive Chef: James Walt

BEARFOOT BISTRO

After a day of outdoor exhilaration, be it skiing and snowboarding in winter or golfing, hiking and mountain biking in summer, you deserve an evening with equally spectacular fine food and wine. Food critics will suggest dining at Bearfoot Bistro and you will not go wrong to follow their advice. Under the guidance of executive chef Brock Windsor, the staff creates everything from scratch using only premium ingredients. You will find dishes such as Seared Ahi Tuna with Celeriac Cake and Clam Jus, Rack of Lamb in a Portabello Crust with Chicory Jus, Eggplant Gnocchi and Grilled Vegetables or Bearfoot's Chocolate Symphony — a selection of French and Belgian chocolate creations for two. Compliment the meal with a selection of wine or champagne from sommelier Kirk Shaw's extensive wine cellar which contains over 14,000 bottles (1,300 labels) of fine Pacific Northwest and international wines.

Bearfoot Bistro entertains with live jazz nightly in winter and weekends in summer. For those who do not participate in wild outdoor sports or for the sport enthusiast who also loves to cook, Bearfoot offers group culinary classes and individual "Chef-for-a-Day" opportunities. Chef-for-a-Day allows participants to shadow the chefs in the Bearfoot kitchen for one to five days, culminating in a dining experience with founder Andre Saint-Jacques and staff.

4121 Village Green
Whistler, BC V0N 1B4
Telephone: (604) 932-3433
E-mail: info@bearfootbistro.com
Web site: www.bearfootbistro.com (web site reservations taken)
Open year-round • Dinner daily
Restaurateur: Andre Saint-Jacques • Executive Chef: Brock Windsor • Chef de Cuisine: Sheldon Prodanuk

CHEF BERNARD'S CAFÉ

Bernard Casavant has always been a staunch promoter of all things local: wine, meat, seafood, produce, Pacific Northwest cuisine, other restaurants and other chefs, whether they be seasoned veterans or eager apprentices. A former executive chef at Chateau Whistler, Bernard stepped across the square and opened a group of establishments well loved by locals and tourists alike. Chef Bernard's Café is small, bustling and always filled with patrons be it breakfast at 7:00 a.m. or dinner until 9:00 p.m. Specialties include his famous cinnamon pecan buns, Carrot and Brie Soup, organic sandwiches and salads complimented with his personal line of Ciao-Thyme condiments. Chef Bernard's offers al fresco dining in summer and a full catering service.

On site you will also find B.B.K.'s Pub, a totally smoke-free pub with only 24 seats, which offers dinner nightly and Blackcomb Beer and Wine Store which features a variety of speculative wines not found in the government liquor stores.

4573 Chateau Boulevard
Whistler, BC V0N 1B4
Telephone: (604) 932-7051
E-mail: bbks@whooshnet.com
Open year-round • Breakfast, lunch and dinner daily
Owner/Executive Chef: Bernard Casavant

EDGEWATER LODGE

It is difficult to imagine a setting more idyllic than that occupied by Edgewater Lodge on the northern outskirts of Whistler. The inn is surrounded by towering snow-capped mountains and borders a glacially-fed green lake and a river wistfully named the River of Golden Dreams. You will wake up in the morning to a vista that is simply magnificent.

The retreat offers lodging with breakfast in 12 rooms, all with waterside and mountain views. Guests may enjoy the on-site spa and canoeing and kayaking activities, as well as golf at the adjacent Nicklaus North Golf Course. Other winter and summer attractions of the Whistler area are within close proximity.

The dining room overlooks the lake and mountains and is enclosed on three sides by large windows, making you feel at one with nature. Executive chef Thomas Piekarski prepares classic gourmet cuisine, often exercising his special flair for sauces. The tender venison is farm-raised at the lodge's own ranch north of Whistler, and local ingredients are featured in season.

8841 Highway 99
Whistler, BC V0N 1B0
Telephone: (604) 932-0688 or 1-888-870-9065
E-mail: jays@whooshnet.com
Web site: www.edgewater-lodge.com
Open year-round • Dinner daily (reservations suggested)
Owner/Proprietor: Jay Symons • Executive Chef: Thomas Piekarski

breakfast, lunch and dinner in a unique market-style atmosphere that features specialty pizzas, pastas, soups, salads, sandwiches and comfort food entrees.

4599 Chateau Boulevard
Whistler, BC V0N 1B4
Telephone: The Wildflower: (604) 938-2033
Portobello: (604) 938-2040
Hotel: (604) 938-8000
E-mail: chateauwhistlerresort@fairmont.com
Web site: www.fairmont.com
Open year-round • Breakfast, lunch and dinner daily
Restaurant Manager: Fergus O'Halloran • Executive Chef: Vincent Stufano

THE FAIRMONT CHÂTEAU WHISTLER
Including
THE WILDFLOWER
PORTOBELLO

The Fairmont Château Whistler, a massive stone structure featuring 550 guestrooms and suites, is located at the base of Blackcomb and Whistler Mountains. Winter amenities include slope-side access for downhill skiing and snowboarding, snowmobiling, Nordic and heli-skiing, skating and snowshoeing. In summer, guests may enjoy golfing at four designer golf courses, mountain biking, hiking, swimming, fishing, tennis, sightseeing and other activities. The hotel houses a world-class convention centre, state-of-the-art health club and full-service spa.

The hotel's two restaurants, under the direction of executive chef Vincent Stufano, offer guests fine cuisine with a healthy attitude. Chef Stufano's philosophy is to use fresh meats and seafood together with regional, organic produce; and turn them into dishes that let the natural flavours express themselves. The Wildflower offers breakfast, lunch (in season) and fine evening dining with an elegant mountain lodge ambience. The more casual Portobello offers

LA RUA RESTAURANTE

La Rua Restaurante is situated at the base of Blackcomb Mountain in Whistler's Upper Village of . Owner Mario Enero's Spanish background and tastes inspire the restaurant's casual Mediterranean ambience. The name Rua refers to the arched entrances in the old towns and villages of Enero's homeland, and he carries this inviting theme throughout the eatery.

The main dining room, with its terra cotta tiled floor, crisp linens and large windows, offers a good vantage point to watch the hustle and bustle of activity at the base of the mountain. Stroll through another arch to enter the romantic Mural Dining Room, with its warm, soft colours and a painted mural wall. In summer, the restaurant opens for patio dining.

Executive chef R. D. Stewart is a master at creating European cuisine with definite Pacific Northwest undertones. Dishes may include mussels roasted with black beans, ginger and cracked chilies, pappardelle pasta with pan seared strips of tenderloin, roasted garlic and shallots in a herb lie, pork tenderloin with a Mandarin honey glaze followed by a dessert of warm hazelnut coffee cake with glazed pear, praline and caramel.

La Rua offers guests a core selection of superb wines chosen for their value and harmony with the cuisine. La Rua's Reserve Lists feature a specialized selection of fine wines from both Old and New World sources. La Rua Restaurante is frequently featured as one of the top mountain resort restaurants in North America.

Whistler Upper Village (located in the Chamois Hotel)
4557 Blackcomb Way
Whistler, BC V0N 1B0
Telephone: (604) 932-5011
Web site: www.larua-restaurante.com
Open year-round • Dinner daily
Proprietor: Mario Enero • Executive Chef: R. D. Stewart

QUATTRO AT WHISTLER

Many successful Vancouver restaurants have established offshoots in the Whistler resort area and diners familiar with the parent restaurants expect the same excellent fare and service there. They are not disappointed in the Corsi family's Quattro at Whistler, located in Pinnacle Hotel and partnered with Corsi's well-known Quattro on Fourth, in Kitsilano, and Gusto di Quattro in North Vancouver. All three restaurants specialize in the cuisine of central Italy.

As you step through the doors at Quattro, warm herbal aromas from the kitchen beckon you to relax in a setting of mature dark woods, white dishes, crisp linens and sparkling glass. Executive chef Jeremie Trottier follows the Italian tradition of simple preparation using only the freshest, healthiest products available. The aim is to let the ingredients speak for themselves. Diners may choose from a variety of appetizers, soups, salads, pastas, meat and seafood entrées and desserts, complemented by wines from the restaurant's extensive wine list.

4319 Main Street (located in the Pinnacle Hotel)
Whistler, BC V0N 1B4
Telephone: (604) 905-4844
E-mail: whistler@quattrorestaurants.com
Web site: www.quattrorestaurants.com (web site reservations taken)
Open year-round • Dinner daily (summer); Wednesday to Sunday (winter)
Partners: Antonio and Patrick Corsi • General Manager: Jay Paré • Executive Chef: Jeremie Trottier

RIMROCK CAFÉ

Rimrock Café is located on Route 99, the Sea to Sky Highway, just south of Whistler Village. Co-owners Bob Dawson and Rolf Gunther pride themselves on the quality of their restaurant's cuisine, which consistently earns Rimrock reviews as one of the premier restaurants in the Whistler area. They specialize in fresh seafood expertly prepared, with sauces and accompaniments that highlight but never detract from the delicate ocean flavour. Equal attention is given to the soups, salads, meat entrées and desserts featured on the menu.

Rimrock provides elegant dining in a warm casual setting. The atmosphere is relaxed, and expert service ensures a comfortable evening after an exhausting day of winter or summer sports. To avoid disappointment, make early reservations at this popular restaurant.

2117 Whistler Road
P.O. Box 1055
Whistler, BC V0N 1B0
Telephone: (604) 932-5565 or 1-877-932-5589
E-mail: inquiries@rimrockwhistler.com
Web site: www.rimrockwhistler.com
Open year-round except mid-Oct to mid-Nov • Dinner daily
Chef/Owner: Rolf Gunther • Manager/Owner: Bob Dawson

TRATTORIA DI UMBERTO RESTAURANT

Trattoria di Umberto, the more casual of Umberto Menghi's two eateries in the village of Whistler, captures the essence of a true Italian trattoria. Here you can enjoy home cooking away from home in a milieu that is as comfortable as dining around the kitchen table. The eatery is warm and inviting, with its rustic-coloured walls, unique artwork, crisp white linens and heavenly aromas emanating from the kitchen.

Trattoria di Umberto is well suited to a relaxing lunch break during the day or a soothing evening meal after a day of sports excitement. The menu includes a variety of authentic Italian appetizers, soups, salads, pastas, seafood and meat entrées and daily dessert selections, all complemented by a fine selection of wines and liqueurs. For a more formal dining experience visit Menghi's, Il Caminetto at 4242 Village Stroll.

4417 Sundial Place
Whistler, BC VON 1B0
Telephone: (604) 932-5858
E-mail: trattoria@umberto.com
Web site: www.umberto.com (web site reservations taken)
Open year-round • Lunch and dinner daily
Owner: Umberto Menghi

VAL D'ISÈRE RESTAURANT

It may seem a little presumptuous to open a restaurant under the shadow of Whistler and Blackcomb Mountains that's named after a famous peak in the French Alps. But owner Roland Pfaff can be forgiven for he brings us more than a name — he also shares with us his wonderful French cuisine. It is easy to see that Pfaff enjoys life and food and that his main goal is to create something special for his guests. Val d'Isère is situated in the heart of Whistler's buzzing Town Plaza and is a great spot to people watch.

Pfaff cooks in the traditional French manner but is not averse to creating unique cuisine with the addition of local specialties. His Roasted Veal is served with a sauce of Vancouver Island morel mushrooms, and he creates a delicious Dungeness Crab Ravioli Gratin with Smoked Salmon Sauce using local seafood. Make sure you leave room for Val d'Isère's famous desserts, such as Pink Lady Apple Tart with Grand Marnier and Cider Pecan Cream or the spectacular Study in Chocolate. The wine list is extensive and well chosen to accent the cuisine.

Bear Lodge at the Town Plaza
#8-4314 Main Street
Whistler, BC VON 1B0
Telephone: (604) 932-4666
E-mail: valdiser@telus.net
Web site: www.valdisere-restaurant.com
Open year-round • Lunch & dinner: June to mid-October
Dinner: Mid-October to June
Manager: Daniel Liddy • Owner/Executive Chef: Roland Pfaff

7 C's Spice Blend, 99
1912 Scallop and Prawn Sauté, 77

Aerie Resort, 41, 82, 106, 118-19, 145
Al Granchio (Black Squid Pasta with Dungeness Crab Sauce), 80
All Seasons Café, 132
Almond Crackers, 113
Almond Ginger-Crusted Chilean Sea Bass with Orange
    Lime Beurre Blanc, 85
Amphora Tapas Bar, 47, 65, 117, 134
Appetizers, 11-26
    Baked Artichokes with Garlic Mayonnaise, 23
    Cucumber garnish, 31
    Egg Crepes, 24
    Fresh-Shucked Pacific Oysters with West Coast Splash, 13
    Garlic Mayonnaise, 23
    Grilled Fanny Bay Oysters with Smoked Paprika
    Mayonnaise, 12
    Habañero Mayonnaise, 20
    Lemongrass Cream, 21
    Lime Sesame Dressing, 22
    Miso Soy Dressing, 19
    Nori-Wrapped Dungeness Crab Cakes with Lemongrass
        Cream, 20
    Pan-Seared Camembert with Spicy Cranberry Sauce, 16
    Rare Ahi Tuna with Asian Papaya Slaw, 22
    Red Shiso and Sesame Pancakes, 19
    Sushi Rice, 25
    Thai Curry Beef with Ginger Aïoli and Avocado on Hearts
        of Romaine, 14-15
    Tojo's Golden Roll, 24
    West Coast Splash, 13
    Wild B.C. Sockeye Salmon on Red Shiso and Sesame
        Pancakes, 18-19
Araxi, 153
Arrowleaf Cellars, 76
Asparagus, Sweet Pepper and Tomato Salad, 92

Baked Artichokes with Garlic Mayonnaise, 23
Balsamic Sauce, 108
Balsamic Sesame Vinaigrette, 46
Beach Side Cafe, 12, 32
Bearfoot Bistro, 154
Bin 941 and Bin 942 Tapas Parlours, 60, 83, 108-09, 138
Bishop's Restaurant, 110, 121, 138-39
Boca Negra, 128
Borgo Antico Ristorante, 51, 69
Braised Rabbit with Wild Mushrooms, Fresh Herbs and
    Mascarpone Polenta, 72
Branzio Alla Crosta (Crusted Sea Bass), 84
Breakfast, Lunch and Tea, 101-13
    Almond Crackers, 113
    Chanterelle and Sweet Corn Risotto, 110
    Chateau Whistler Granola, 103
    Empress Scones, 112
    Frittata Trattoria, 104
    Mount Currie Rhubarb and Sweet Ginger Chutney, 111
    Orange Cardamon French Toast, 102
    Portobello Mushroom Cutlets with Balsamic Sauce and
        Roasted Baby Vegetables, 108-09
    Spring Mushroom Cannelloni, 106
    Summerhill Smoked Salmon Eggs Benedict, 105
    Sun-Dried Tomato Risotto, 107
Brioche and 7 C's Spice-Crusted Pacific Lingcod, 98-99

C Restaurant, 98, 139
Cafe Brio, 146

Cambozola Caldo Con Crostini, 52
Camille's Restaurant, 146
Caprese Salad of Tomatoes and Bocconcini, 51
Caramelized Apple and Phyllo Tower with Crème Anglaise
    and Easy Caramel Sauce, 126-27
Carrot and Sage Velouté, 41
Cayman Island Chowder, 35
Cedar Creek Estate, 88, 95, 134-35
Cedar-Infused B.C. Salmon with Onion Confit and
    Hazelnut and Balsamic Vinaigrette, 90-91
Cellar Door Bistro & Catering, 55, 61, 135
Cellar Door Caesar, 55
Champagne Sabayon, 129
Chanterelle and Sweet Corn Risotto, 110
Chanterelle-Stuffed Venison Medallions with Three-
    Peppercorn Soy Vinaigrette, 62
Chateau Whistler Granola, 103
Chanterelle Paté, 62
Chef Bernard's Café, 154
Chicken Curry, 64
Chive Butter Sauce, 76
Chocolate Terrine, 124
Cin Cin, 23, 92, 139-140
Cin Cin Poached Salmon with Sorrel Sauce, 92-93
Cinnamon Chili Rub Flank Steak, 60
Circolo, 144
Citrus Curd, 118
Coconut Milk and Masala Mussels, 83
Country Squire, 29, 30, 31, 129
Cranberry-Stuffed Pork Tenderloin in Phyllo, 68
Cranberry Vinegar, 87
Cranberry Vinegar Sauce, 87
Cream of Chanterelle Soup with Blueberry Crème Fraîche, 37
Creamy Parmesan Polenta, 71
Crème Anglaise, 126
Cucumber garnish, 31

Delight of the King, 131
Desserts, 115-31
    Boca Negra, 128
    Caramelized Apple and Phyllo Tower with Crème
        Anglaise and Easy Caramel Sauce, 126-27
    Chocolate Terrine, 124
    Delight of the King, 131
    Frangelico Mousse with Champagne Sabayon, 129
    Fresh Berries with Ginger-Scented Mascarpone, Citrus
        Curd and Pistachio Tuile towers, 118-19
    Nanaimo Bars, 125
    Rhubarb Upside-Down Cakes, 121
    Stilton Cheesecake with Rhubarb Compote, 122
    Stone Fruit Clafouti with Toasted Hazelnuts, 117
    Sunburnt Lemon Pie, 116
    Warm Pecan Pie with Vanilla Bean Ice Cream, 130
    Warm Rain Forest Crunch Banana with Hot Chocolate
        Sauce, 120
Diva at the Met, 18, 81, 122, 140
Domaine de Chaberton Estates, 98
Double-Strength Chicken Stock, 30

Eagle's Eye Restaurant, 132-33
Easy Caramel Sauce, 127
Edgewater Lodge, 16, 46, 70, 154-55
Edgewater Marinated Venison Medallions, 70
Edgewater Salad, 46
Egg Crepes, 24
Empress Scones, 112
Entrées. See Meat Entrées

Fairmont Château Whistler, 155
Fairmont Empress Hotel, 28, 64, 112, 125, 146-47
Fairmont Hot Springs Resort, 133
Fiddler's Green Restaurant, 133
Frangelico Mousse with Champagne Sabayon, 129
Fresco Restaurant, 135
Fresh Berries with Ginger-Scented Mascarpone, Citrus Curd
    and Pistachio Tuile Towers, 118-19
Fresh Ginger Juice Sauce, 96
Fresh-Shucked Pacific Oysters with West Coast Splash, 13
Frittata Trattoria, 104

Garlic Mayonnaise, 23
Gehringer Brothers Estate Winery, 63
Ginger-Scented Mascarpone Mousse, 118
Good Life Bookstore Café, 67
Good Night Salmon, 97
Grainy Mustard Bill Beurre Blanc, 68
Gray Monk Estate Winery, 71
Green and Yellow Bean Salad with a Warm Bacon Vinaigrette, 47
Grilled Fanny Bay Oysters with Smoked Paprika Mayonnaise, 12
Grilled Fillet of Wild Salmon with Summer Salsa, 94
Grilled Halibut T-Bone with Summer Vegetable Salad and
    Crème Fraîche Mousse, 82
Grilled Vegetables, 63
Grotto, 54, 86
Grotto-style Sesame Sauce, 86

Habañero Mayonnaise, 20
Hainle Vineyards Estate Winery, 47, 65, 117, 134
Hastings House, 147
Hay-Roasted Fraser Valley Poussins with Creamy Parmesan
    Polenta, 71
Hazelnut Vinaigrette, 91
Herald Street Caffe, 62, 96, 120, 148
Herbed Chicken Stock, 106
Herbed Croutons, 55
Historic 1912 Restaurant and Country Inn, 77
Hollandaise Sauce, 105
Honey Wine Sauce, 66
Hot-and-Sour Soup, 38
Hot Chocolate Sauce, 120

Il Giardino and Umberto's, 63, 144
Indonesian Sweet Potato, Coconut and Peanut Soup, 36
Inniskillin Okanagan Vineyards, 80

J & J Wonton Noodle House, 148
Jackson-Triggs Vintners, 87, 92

Kerin Mandarin, 140
Kettle Valley Winery, 83
Kingfisher Oceanside Restaurant, 148

La Frenz Vineyard and Winery, 96
La Rua Restaurante, 56, 76, 155-56
Lake Breeze Wines, 69, 97
Latch Country Inn, 50, 94, 130
Le Crocodile, 39, 140-41
Leek and Fennel Soup, 29
Lemon Oil, 79
Lemon Potatoes, 76
Lemongrass Cream, 21
L'Emotion Restaurant, 141
Lime Sesame Dressing, 22
Lobster Bisque, 28
Lobster Stock, 28

Lumière Restaurant, 141
Lunch. See Breakfast, Lunch and Tea

Mahle House Restaurant, 40, 72, 78, 128, 149
Mascarpone Polenta, 73
Meat Entrées, 59-73
    Braised Rabbit with Wild Mushrooms, Fresh Herbs and
        Mascarpone Polenta, 72
    Cranberry-Stuffed Pork Tenderloin in Phyllo, 68
    Chanterelle-Stuffed Venison Medallions with Three-
        Peppercorn Soy Vinaigrette, 62
    Chicken Curry, 64
    Cinnamon Chili Rub Flank Steak, 60
    Coq Au Vin with Braised Greens, 65
    Edgewater Marinated Venison Medallions, 70
    Hay-Roasted Fraser Valley Poussins with Creamy
        Parmesan Polenta, 71
    Herb-Crusted Rack of Lamb, 66
    Roasted Garlic Chicken and Grilled Vegetables, 63
    Smoked Pork Tenderloin with Oven-Dried Damson Plums, 61
    Smoked Salmon-Stuffed Chicken Breast in Phyllo with
        Sour Cherry Ginger Glaze, 67
    Veal and Lemon Caper Sauce, 69
Memphis Blues Barbecue House, 141-42
Miso Soy Dressing, 19
Mission Hill Family Estate, 62, 84, 86
Mount Boucherie Estate Winery, 85
Mount Currie Rhubarb and Sweet Ginger Chutney, 111

Nanaimo Bars, 125
Naramata Heritage Inn and Spa, 135-36
Noggin's Chowder, 34
Nori-Wrapped Dungeness Crab Cakes with Lemongrass
    Cream, 20

Old House Restaurant, 68, 149
Old Vines Patio at Quail's Gate Estate Winery, 136
Onion Confit, 90
Orange Cardamom French Toast, 102
Orange Lime Beurre Blanc, 85
Oritalia, 14, 20, 102

Pacific Oyster Stew, 42
Pan-Charred Rare Tuna with Grotto-Style Sesame Sauce, 86
Pan-Seared Camembert with Spicy Cranberry Sauce, 16
Pistachio Tuiles, 119
Portobello Mushroom Cutlets with Balsamic Sauce and
    Roasted Baby Vegetables, 108-09
Potato Artichoke Hash, 81

Quail's Gate Estate Winery, 64, 72, 90, 136
Quattro at Whistler, 80, 84, 113, 124, 156

Rabbit Stock, 72
Raincity Grill, 142
RainCoast Café, 13, 36, 150
Rare Ahi Tuna with Asian Papaya Slaw, 22
Raspberry Vinaigrette, 48
rebar modern food, 150
Red Shiso and Sesame Pancakes, 19
Rhubarb Upside-Down Cakes, 121
Rimrock Café, 22, 37, 85, 156
Roasted Baby Vegetables, 109
Roasted Garlic Chicken and Grilled Vegetables, 65
Roasted Sweet Pepper Sauce, 84

Salads, 45-56
  Asparagus, Sweet Pepper and Tomato Salad, 92
  Cambazola Caldo Con Crostini, 52
  Caprese Salad of Tomatoes and Bocconcini, 51
  Cellar Door Caesar, 55
  Edgewater Salad, 46
  Green and Yellow Bean Salad with a Warm Bacon
    Vinaigrette, 47
  Spicy Mesclun with Avocado, Mango and Stilton Cheese, 48
  Spinach Salad With Honey Dressing and Pancetta Fetta
    Tuques, 56
  Spinnakers Mixed Greens with Raspberry Vinaigrette, 48
  Summer Vegetable Salad, 82
  Sunomono Salad, 54
Salty's Beach House Restaurant, 35, 136
Sandhill Wines, 60
Sautéed Sea Asparagus, 90
Scallion Oil, 81
Scallops Napoleon, 78-79
Seafood Entrées
  1912 Scallop and Prawn Sauté, 77
  Al Granchio (Black Squid Pasta with Dungeness Crab Sauce), 80
  Almond Ginger-Crusted Chilean Sea Bass with Orange
    Lime Beurre Blanc, 85
  Branzio Alla Crosta (Crusted Sea Bass), 84
  Brioche and 7 C's Spice-Crusted Pacific Lingcod, 98-99
  Cedar-Infused B.C. Salmon with Onion Confit and
    Hazelnut and Balsamic Vinaigrette, 90-91
  Cin Cin Poached Salmon with Sorrel Sauce, 92-93
  Coconut Milk and Masala Mussels, 83
  Good Night Salmon, 97
  Grilled Fillet of Wild Salmon with Summer Salsa, 94
  Grilled Halibut T-Bone with Summer vegetable Salad and
    Crème Fraîche Mousse, 82
  Halibut Poêle with Lemon Potatoes and Chive Butter Sauce, 76
  Pan-Charred Rare Tuna with Grotto-Style Sesame Sauce, 86
  Scallops Napoleon, 78-79
  Seared Medallion of Smoked Alaskan Black Cod with
    Potato Artichoke Hash and Scallion Oil, 81
  Smoked Black Alaska Cod with Grainy Mustard Dill
    Beurre Blanc, 88
  Sooke Harbour House Steamed Skate Wing with
    Cranberry Vinegar Sauce, 87
  Stilton-crusted Salmon Fillet with Warm Caper Relish and
    Sweet Soy Glaze, 95
  Wild Salmon and Sorrel with Fresh Ginger Juice Sauce, 96
Seared Medallion of Smoked Alaskan Black Cod with
  Potato Artichoke Hash and Scallion Oil, 81
Seasons Restaurant, 42, 88, 116, 142
Sherried Shiitake and Brown Mushroom Confit, 78
Shoal Harbour Inn and Latch Dining Rooms, 150-51
Simply Thai, 142-43
Smoked Black Alaska Cod with Grainy Mustard Dill Beurre
  Blanc, 88
Smoked Gouda Soup, 40
Smoked Pork Tenderloin with Oven-Dried Damson Plums, 61
Smoked Salmon-Stuffed Chicken Breast in Phyllo with Sour
  Cherry Ginger Glaze, 67
Sooke Harbour House, 87, 151
Sooke Harbour House Steamed Skate Wing with Cranberry
  Vinegar Sauce, 87
Sorrel Sauce, 93
Soups, 27-42
  Carrot and Sage Velouté, 41
  Cayman Island Chowder, 35
  Cream of Chanterelle Soup with Blueberry Crème Fraîche, 37
  Double-Strength Chicken Stock, 30

  Hot-and-Sour Soup, 38
  Indonesian Sweet Potato, Coconut and Peanut Soup, 36
  Leek and Fennel Soup, 29
  Lobster Bisque, 28
  Lobster Stock, 28
  Noggin's Chowder, 34
  Pacific Oyster Stew, 42
  Smoked Gouda Soup, 40
  Sweet Pea Soup with Crème Fraîche and Hand-Peeled
    Shrimp, 32
  Sweet Red Pepper Soup, 31
  Vichyssoise with Lobster medallions, 39
Spicy Cranberry Sauce, 16
Spicy Mesclun with Avocado, Mango and Stilton Cheese, 50
Spinach Salad With Honey Dressing and Pancetta Fetta
  Tuques, 56
Spinnakers Brewpub & Guesthouse, 34, 38, 48, 151-52
Spinnakers Mixed Greens with Raspberry Vinaigrette, 48
Spring Mushroom Cannelloni, 106
Stag's Hollow Winery and Vineyard, 67
Stilton Cheesecake with Rhubarb Compote, 122
Stilton-crusted Salmon Fillet with Warm Caper Relish and
  Sweet Soy Glaze, 95
Stone Fruit Clafouti with Toasted Hazelnuts, 117
Strand's Old House Restaurant, 133
Sumac Ridge Estate Winery, 61, 66, 70, 77, 82, 104
Summer Salsa, 94
Summer Vegetable Salad, 82
Summerhill Estate Winery, 78, 105, 137
Summerhill Smoked Salmon Eggs Benedict, 105
Sun-Dried Tomato Risotto, 107
Sunburnt Lemon Pie, 116
Sunomono Salad, 54
Sunset Veranda Restaurant, 105
Sushi Rice, 25
Sweet Pea Soup with Crème Fraîche and Hand-Peeled Shrimp, 32
Sweet Red Pepper Soup, 31
Sweet Soy Glaze, 95

Tea. See Breakfast, Lunch and Tea
Teahouse Restaurant at Kelowna Land & Orchard, 137
Teahouse Restaurant in Stanley Park, 66, 131, 143
Thai Curry Beef with Ginger Aïoli and Avocado on Hearts
  of Romaine, 14-15
Tinhorn Creek Vineyards, 68, 94
Tojo's Restaurant, 24, 97, 143-44
Tomatillo Emulsion, 99
Township 7 Vineyards, 81
Trattoria di Umberto Restaurant, 52, 104, 157

Val d'Isère Restaurant, 90, 107, 157
Veal and Lemon Caper Sauce, 69
Vichyssoise with Lobster Medallions, 39

Warm Caper Relish, 95
Warm Pecan Pie with Vanilla Bean Ice Cream, 130
Warm Rain Forest Crunch Banana with Hot Chocolate
  Sauce, 120
Wesley Street restaurant, 95, 126-27
West Coast Splash, 13
White Chocolate Cream, 128
Wickaninnish Inn & Pointe Restaurant, 152
Wild B.C. Sockeye Salmon on Red Shiso and Sesame
  Pancakes, 18-19
Wild Salmon and Sorrel with Fresh Ginger Juice Sauce, 96
Wildflower Restaurant, 71, 103, 111
Williams Inn, 137